Sadhu, Beware!

A New Approach to Renunciation

Sadhu, Beware!

FEB 2023

A New Approach to Renunciation

by Swami Kriyananda

CRYSTAL CLARITY PUBLISHERS
NEVADA CITY, CALIFORNIA

ISBN: 1-56589-214-3
1 3 5 7 9 10 8 6 4 2

Printed in India

Crystal Clarity Publishers
14618 Tyler Foote Road
Nevada City, CA 95959

800.424.1055
www.crystalclarity.com

Library of Congress CIP data available

Contents

I

Ananda Sangha

In the normal course of events, a renunciate order defines itself by the contrast it forms with society as a whole. A renunciate is, or should be, wholly dedicated to seeking and serving God. Most people in society are dedicated to worldly pursuits and ego-gratification.

In Ananda Sangha this contrast is less definite, for *all* who join Ananda do so in order to seek and serve God. They should already understand, moreover, their need to transcend ego-consciousness by doing God's will rather than their own. Whether or not they embrace formal renunciation, the gratification they are taught to seek is not of the ego: It is in God. Thus, within Ananda Sangha the contrasts between those who embrace formal renunciation and those who do not are less distinct. For this reason they need to be spelled out with extra care. For this reason also, much—and perhaps most—of what follows will be useful to all the members of Ananda Sangha.

Years ago, when the distinction between the two groups was not sufficiently clear, I attempted to create a renunciate order. That attempt failed. It failed because the monks and nuns had no choice, given the way our community operated, but to mix freely with one another and, indeed, with the whole community. Segregating them simply was not possible. Human nature, in addition to their own past social conditioning, conspired to make it impossible for them, especially the younger ones, to ignore the natural attraction the sexes feel toward each other. Thus, the ship of renunciation at Ananda Village foundered, as indeed I had feared it might. There was nothing I could do about it. It was the circumstances that dictated the conclusion.

There is something in the air, moreover, in modern times that seems to militate against the monastic way of life. Everywhere—even in India, which is well known for its *sadhus* or holy men—the trend seems to be away from world-renunciation. In Italy, huge monasteries that once housed hundreds stand empty. People throughout the world seem to feel that God not only can be sought in the family, but should be: that this way is preferable to renunciation of a normal life. Lahiri Mahasaya himself, in the incarnation we know, lived as a householder. Most or all of Paramhansa Yogananda's most advanced disciples, moreover, were or had been householders.

Is this trend away from monasticism a response to some deeply felt need in society? Until the home life we now know can be more spiritualized, fewer people, I think, will feel the call to renunciation. This feeling has arisen within me after many years of traveling through the world. Wherever I've gone, I have heard the same feeling expressed, sometimes consciously, and sometimes indirectly. It seems to me that there will be no serious general movement toward the path of renunciation until this ideal receives wider support. Indeed, too many people today seem to be uncommitted to anything. This lack is suggested everywhere. It is particularly evident in the large number of divorces nowadays.

People must learn to take greater responsibility for their lives. Today, too many think instead that the purpose of human existence is sense gratification and self-aggrandizement.

Ananda Sangha communities have been created to build a solid basis of spirituality for people at all stages of life. Only on such a basis can the superstructure of real commitment to God be erected. Unfortunately, divorces do occur at Ananda also, though not nearly so many as in society at large. There would be fewer, surely, were society in general completely stable. Ananda is a steppingstone to that stability. At Ananda, there is at least a seriousness of spiritual purpose that one rarely encounters in the world. Ananda Sangha has been inspiring people everywhere to develop a life of serious commitment to God.

Paramhansa Yogananda once stated, "If you marry as a necessity, you will have to reincarnate again to reach the point where you can live for God alone." The key words in that statement are not, "If you marry," but, "If you marry *as a necessity.*" What did he mean by that word, "necessity"? Obviously he wasn't thinking of parental and societal expectations. He could have had only one meaning: "*If you marry with the perception that you need human love for your fulfillment.*" When I mentioned that the Master's most highly advanced disciples were householders, it must be understood also that those householders did find God.

Sister Gyanamata was an outstanding example. She came to live at Mt. Washington only after the death of her husband. And yet—as the Master himself told us—she achieved final liberation in this life.

Ultimately, what I think the Master had to mean by his statement was that the devotee must reach the point where he loves God alone, and needs no human being to fulfill his natural longing for love.

The Ananda Sangha communities have reached a point in their maturity, I think, where it may be time seriously to consider creating, within the total definition of the Sangha, an order of renunciates for men and for women.

I doubt that it has ever been possible to develop a flourishing renunciate order *within* society at large. Renunciates need to define their way of life clearly, lest the differences become blurred with the kind of conditioning that most people accept as the norm. As Yogananda put it, "Environment is stronger than will power."

It is a lamentable, but unfortunately common, mistake of renunciates to pride themselves on being more spiritually qualified than "householders." I would like at the outset of this paper, therefore, to emphasize that *the only valid definition of renunciation is the renunciation of ego-identification.* The renunciate must offer his entire being into the Infinite Self. Only when complete freedom has been achieved from ego-limitation can God be realized. At that point, indeed, there is nothing left to be renounced!

The first quality to be considered, therefore, is the renunciation of ego-attachment.

II

Humility

What is humility? The first point to under-stand is that humility is *not* self-abasement. To lower oneself is an indication, not of ego-transcendence, but of preoccupation with the little self. One who bows to the ground and throws dust on his head concentrates on dust and on his own head. Implicit in this attitude is a distorted kind of self-involvement: ego-centeredness. Self-involvement is, in fact, simply the negative aspect of *egotism*, or arrogance.

True humility is *self-forgetfulness*, leading to *self-transcendence*. By self-forgetfulness, therefore, I don't mean stumbling about, bumping into tables or other objects because one is insufficiently aware of his body! Nor do I mean other symptoms of lessened perception, such as absent-mindedness or carelessness, which foolish critics—trying to prick holes in our teaching because they find it inconvenient—might assume from what I've recommended. All I mean is not to refer back to oneself anything that happens: for example, not to say such things as, "*I* did that. *I* didn't get the attention I deserved. Why did this happen to *me*?"

Some renunciates practice humility by self-effacement. This is a valid, though not a universally desirable, method. Not everyone who strives for self-transcendence can achieve this end by that route. Others who aspire to the same goal may be naturally more expansive, and perhaps more creative. There is no need to equate an expansive outlook with egotism. For expansive people, self-effacement would entail, rather, a negative use of their energy. In focusing on self-denial, they might only expend energy uselessly in suppression of their natural ebullience.

People are uniquely themselves. What is right for one person might be wrong for another. A mistake often made in traditional monasteries is to try to fit all their members into the same mold. Humility defined in such ways as a downward gaze is negative. It might be spiritually helpful for some people, but others might find it merely suppressive. There are many spiritual seekers for whom it would be useless to try to suppress their natural expansiveness and creativity. What they need, rather, is simply to release their energy in expansion. As the Bhagavad Gita states, "Of what avail is suppression?" People who are expansive by nature find it more relaxing to let their energy expand than by attempting to bottle it up. Introvertive types, on the other hand, become tense at the very thought of extroversion.

In expansion, however, one must always hold the thought, "God is the Doer." One will not gain spiritually if what he tries to expand is his ego.

The spiritual path may be summed up as an effort to attain Self-realization in infinity. God is our true Self. It is from His consciousness that everyone and everything was manifested.

The ego will never, and *can* never, be annihilated—not even in infinite consciousness. Self-annihilation is not the issue. The drop retains its reality even after becoming absorbed in the ocean. Paramhansa Yogananda in his poem "Samadhi" used the simile of the ocean and the waves. "I, the Cosmic Sea," he wrote, "watch the little ego floating in Me." This consciousness of being merged in God is not *self-annihilation*; nor is it the destruction of the ego. Rather, it is the realization that the ego, too, is a part of Infinity. To merge in God is to free one's self-consciousness from confinement in an ego-prison, but this doesn't mean losing the memory of having been that ego.

To merge in God is freedom absolute. People who view omnipresence with alarm must understand that, in God, *nothing* is lost. For although attachment to the ego is completely transcended, the memory of one's separate, limited identity remains forever a part of eternal omniscience. Thus, the ego can be revived at any time by Cosmic Will, or by the devotional call of sincere devotees. All the waves, and all the drops, *are part of the Infinite Ocean of God.* What the true seeker achieves is *fulfillment in limitless perfection*: including the perfection of self-consciousness in Self-realization.

An interesting point to reflect on is that what appears again, when the individual self is re-manifested, is in fact that *essential being*: that quondam individual. Krishna and Jesus Christ, if lovingly recalled to earth by devotees after thousands of years, *re-manifest as those same entities.* It is not a case of the Absolute simply taking on a similar appearance.

Great masters like Paramhansa Yogananda, though liberated many lifetimes ago, are re-manifested again and again as the same essential beings, with their intrinsic personalities intact. Yogananda, when he incarnated as Arjuna, and again as William the Conqueror, and still again as a Spanish general in the time of the invading Moors, always reappeared as *himself.* Though infinite in consciousness, and merged forever in the ocean of Spirit, the aspect of that infinity that became his ego retains its memory of being that little drop in the infinite ocean.

I have given two accepted ways of achieving infinite consciousness. The first way, I said, is to practice self-effacement. It should be clear from my statement that self-effacement is achieved not by negating one's reality, but by ego-*transcendence.*

The other way to achieve infinite awareness is to offer up to God everything one does, and to think of Him in so doing as the true Doer of everything.

Both ways—inward contraction and outward

2 METHODS

ADD to NOTION ⟶ KEY CONCEPT

expansion—are implied in the advice given by Krishna in the Bhagavad Gita: "*nishkam karma*—action without desire for the fruits of action.*"

Thus, when Paramhansa Yogananda said, as I've quoted him many times in my writings, "The greatest sin is to call yourself a sinner," it is important to understand that what he meant was, "Don't identify yourself with sin. Even when you make mistakes, never say to yourself, '*I am* those mistakes.'"

Many great saints, including Paramhansa Yogananda, have in fact sometimes spoken of themselves as sinners. What they've meant was very different from affirming sinfulness. The distinction lay in their lack of sin-consciousness while making that utterance. In calling themselves sinners, they did so in a spirit of joyful freedom, disclaiming their identity with the ego and affirming, rather, "God is my reality."

One can heap any amount of insults on himself that he likes, if he does so in a spirit of joyful ego-rejection, and if he accepts that his true Self is limitless and divine. This was the attitude of such great saints as Francis of Assisi and Teresa of Avila. They often, and quite cheerfully, derided themselves for their sinfulness, in joyful dismissal of their egos, though never in sorrowful affirmation of any actual evil in themselves.

People who, instead, affirm their own sinfulness give themselves every excuse they need to go right on sinning!

III

Developing Humility

When my brother Bob was three years old, our mother once began a sentence to him with the word, "My. . . ."

"No!" interrupted Bobby: "Not 'my!' 'My's' *me, Wobert.*"

Isn't it strange—indeed, wonderful—how universal is this sense of "I"? The infinite Self never became anything other than Itself. It reflected that Self, like sunlight on countless slivers of glass, in every atom of creation. The Divine Consciousness is the essence of everything in existence.

Scientists have postulated that computers will someday be made so sophisticated that they will become conscious. Out of that consciousness, so goes the postulate, self-consciousness will be manifested. There is a major defect in this expectation: Consciousness is not produced by the brain. It is self-existent, and is what *produces* the brain!

What could be less sophisticated than the earthworm? Yet the worm is self-evidently conscious. If it is touched by anything sharp or hard, it squirms away from the touch. Worms have been taught to follow one path in preference to another, when offered a choice between food at the end of one path and an electric shock at the end of the other.

Everything in existence is conscious. This is true even of rocks, though of course they are not conscious *of being* rocks. Consciousness is the central reality of all existence, both animate and "inanimate." The entire universe is *the product of consciousness*: "center everywhere, circumference nowhere." Self-awareness can expand to infinity from an infinite number of points.

Man's way of creating a thing is outside in. He paints a painting, or carves a statue to give form to his ideas. Pygmalion, in the Greek legend, carved a statue of a woman so beautiful that he fell in love with it. Divine consciousness, symbolized in the goddess Aphrodite, took pity on him and blessed that statue, bringing it to life. That formerly inanimate "it" became a "she." Pygmalion named his living statue Galatea, and married her.

Just think of the infinite variety in human beings: two eyes, a nose, a mouth, yet each one in some marvelous way is quite unique. No two snowflakes, even, are identical.

Each human being has also his own dreams to fulfill: a beautiful home, perhaps; the special contributions he hopes to make to the world; a mate of his own; travel abroad. Above all, there is an indefinable "mood" in his heart that draws him in longing toward some special, personal vision of love and happiness.

A brief snatch of music may awaken this undefined longing in him. A brief smell may stir in him some inchoate memory. Each of the senses exercises on him some special appeal.

How can we rise above our egos? There is so much conspiring to bind us to the ego, and to keep us focused outward through the senses, impelled by our hearts' feelings, to relate to a world which is, in fact, quite imaginary. It seems so clearly, in our imagination, to have a reality of its own! How do we cut away, explode, or beat down into the earth the vague mists of memory which from time to time afford us brief glimpses of something we may hope ever afterward to attain: a longing for what, realistically speaking, may be forever impossible? Often it happens that we cannot even define these fleeting sensations. They enter momentarily into our awareness, swirl about like vapor for a time, then vanish even as we reach out to touch them.

All these things must be renounced if we would know truth and God. One may ask: Why? They are sweet; they fill us with yearning; they may create in us a deep nostalgia. Ah! but when at last we fulfill any one of them, we find that our anticipation has always exceeded the fulfillment. Every fulfillment, indeed, if ever we finally grasp it, turns to dust. *Nothing* ever gives us what we want most from life.

The first duty of every soul is to release the

Sadhu, Beware!

NOTION
1

hold that ego-consciousness has upon it. All other spiritual practices are subservient to this one supreme obligation. I address ego-transcendence, therefore, as the first, and indeed the only, challenge on the spiritual path, whether one be a renunciate, a householder, or living for God in some other way.

I include here a few techniques that will help you in your supremely important efforts to transcend ego-consciousness.

IV

Techniques of Ego-Transcendence

1. When you see something you'd like for yourself, buy it if possible; accept the satisfaction of possessing it. Then, however, give it away with a free heart to someone else.

I did this in Switzerland in 1955, when I was visiting the SRF centers in Europe. I saw a beautiful wood carving of the Madonna for sale. My first thought was how lovely it would be to possess it. The cost, however, was $12, which at the time was much more than twelve dollars are today. To purchase it meant spending four fifths of my monthly monastic allowance. I decided, instead, to buy it as a gift for Daya Mata, SRF's president.

I think I made a good choice. Purchasing that statue gave me the brief joy of possessing it. Next, it gave me the joy of giving it to a friend. And finally, it gave me the joy of seeing it again whenever I got to visit her quarters.

2. When people fail to credit you for something you did and did well, say nothing. In your heart, however, give all the credit to God.

3. When people praise you for any reason, don't accept their praise in your heart. Don't say ungraciously, for example, "It was nothing." That would mean deprecating their good taste and common sense! In fact, it would mean answering a compliment with an insult! Thank them sincerely, instead, but then give the credit to God. Do so in words if you like, but much more importantly, <u>give Him the credit in your heart</u>. Tell yourself, <u>"God is the Doer."</u>

People may remind you, if you say that to them, "Yes, but it takes an *instrument* of God's will to do what you've done so skillfully." True enough, but what does that really mean? Do you want to pride yourself on being a good screwdriver, or hammer?! Move on to some other subject, and be particularly careful, in your *heart*, not to accept the compliment.

4. When someone else gets the credit for something you've done, don't look for a way of letting people know where the credit really belongs. It would be natural enough for you

to do that; you needn't even consider it a fault. Still, don't make too much of it. You will find much greater freedom in your heart if you mentally give all the credit to God.

5. When someone has a good idea that you've had already, it will help you in the practice of humility to tell yourself, "It's the *idea* that counts, not the person who had it." Reply simply, therefore, "That's a good idea. Let's give it a try."

6. If someone scolds you for something you didn't do, you may see some good reason for letting him know that you're not guilty. If it doesn't really matter who did it, however, you will gain more, spiritually, if you say nothing.

7. If you see others eager to air their views, be generous to them: let them speak. Add thoughts of your own only if you see that those others might be interested in what you have to say.

Many people are so convinced of the merit of their own thoughts—a certainty that isn't always backed by real merit!—that even to respond with your own ideas might lower the discussion to a level of competition.

Better, in such a case, to let them have their say. Listen for any benefit you might find in their words and ideas. If you see none (as, let's face it, may often be the case!), show the other person respect, but share the humor of the situation, inwardly, with God.

You might even make a game of it, mentally, by seeing just how boring your interlocutor can be! Some people achieve almost a level of genius in the way they manage to challenge others' patience!

8. If others try to boss you around, and if it doesn't really matter to you one way or another, why not simply go along with the "game"? To do so will increase your sense of inner freedom.

9. Don't try constantly to explain or define for others' gratification who and what you are. Let your actions, and your inner reality, speak for you.

If others misunderstand you, wear their misunderstanding as a mental feather in your cap. Reflect that God alone really understands us, anyway!

10. Never place yourself mentally in competition with others.

11. Never belittle anyone. View all with respect. Release from your heart any desire you may feel to outshine others, or even to shine at all in whatever you do. Do the best you can, always, but give the fruits of your efforts to God.

12. Never try, without some good and definite reason, to justify your actions, ideas, or accomplishments. Whatever you've done, give it mentally to God.

13. Try always to impersonalize your impressions.

I remember once, many years ago, during a gathering of SRF renunciates, someone challenged a particular musical sequence (I don't remember the details) in a chant. A musically gifted nun, present on that occasion, announced firmly, "[This] is how it should go." Another nun answered her, "What makes you so certain?" I still remember the ego in the first woman's voice as she replied: "My *ear* tells me!"

This musical nun left her monastic calling soon afterward. After she'd done so, I reflected on that little statement she'd made, and on the way she'd made it. Already, in those four words, were revealed a resurgence in her of ego-consciousness.

Try never, therefore, to make *yourself* the justification for any utterance you make. I don't mean you shouldn't call on your experience. You have a right to that; indeed, it is the only real wisdom you can claim. Never say, however, "I know, owing to my own special talent or insight."

The nun I've mentioned was probably quite right in her assessment. It would have been wiser on her part, however, to answer, "Just listen sensitively. Can't *you* hear the difference?"

14. Always be guided by principles, not by desires. And, especially if you find yourself in a leadership position, never impose your desires or your likes and dislikes on others.

On the other hand, be careful how you let them impose their feelings and wishes on you. As Yogananda said to us, "Don't be a doormat!" Be firm inwardly, while letting principles be as much as possible your guide when making every decision.

15. Stand up for what you feel is right, but try to make it clear always that you are not

trying to impose on anyone values that are merely personal. Base your values on abstract principles.

16. Laugh *with* others, but never *at* them.

17. Try to view with sympathy points of view that differ from your own.

18. Try not to tell stories of which the main point is to make *you* look good.

19. Live always in a spirit of joyful freedom from ego-consciousness.

20. As you practice right principles, people may often express appreciation for the goodness you manifest. Indeed, you will have *become* good. When others show such appreciation, however, remind yourself—and them also, if you like—of an answer Ananda Moyi Ma once gave me. I'd just exclaimed to her, "You are so good!" She replied with a beautiful smile, "It takes goodness to see goodness."

21. It is not humility to tell yourself, "I can't. . . ." Remember, God can do anything. If you give Him the chance, moreover, He can do anything *through you*. Ask Him for the inspiration, the guidance, and the strength to do

tever you must do. As Yogananda put it,
ay in this way: I will reason; I will will; I
will act—but guide Thou my reason, will, and
activity in everything I do."

22. I remember an amusing interchange, years ago: We monks at Mt. Washington liked to play volleyball together. It was good exercise, and also good fun. I must admit, however, that I wasn't much of a player. Cheerfully I kept saying, "Sorry: My fault." One day another of the monks commented with humorous exasperation, "Your humility is inspiring—but *when will you reform*?"

It is perfectly all right, I think, to exchange this sort of badinage. The obvious solution to playing badly, of course, would be—at least if it is important to you—to learn to play well; one should do as well as he can whatever he sets his mind to doing at all.

On the other hand, it would be a waste of time and energy to try to excel at everything. There is no harm in speaking lightly of your ineptitude at certain things. If, on the other hand, you do try to excel, try not to do so *in a competitive spirit*. It is all right to compete with yourself—that is to say, with your own past performances.

A child at an Ananda school many years ago put it perfectly. He had just finished competing in a race involving several schools. Someone asked him, "Did you win?"

"No," he replied, "but I won against myself."

23. Make it a point not to feel badly when you make a mistake. Obviously, it would compound the mistake if you insisted you didn't make it. When you do err, however, acknowledge the error calmly and cheerfully—if not openly before others, then at least inwardly to yourself. (The Master used to say, "Don't tell your faults to others, unless they have spiritual wisdom, lest they hoard up that memory and use it against you sometime out of displeasure with you.")

If possible, don't even say to yourself, "I made this mistake." Say, rather, "The mistake got made." God is the Doer. Give to Him the blame as well as the credit for everything. Then try ever more earnestly to attune your every thought and action to His will.

24. Avoid calling attention to your own cleverness or skill—for instance, by making the

kind of bright remark that is almost always followed by a smirk and a glance around the room for others' approval.

25. In fact, try not to call attention to yourself. If you want to call attention to some thought, try to be sure in your own mind that your desire isn't based on a desire merely to be heard.

26. When you move to a new position in your work or living situation, carry no mental "baggage" with you. Have no expectations. Visualize receiving no recognition for anything you've done, and perhaps being shoved to the bottom of whatever ladder you must now climb. Then visualize yourself accepting that status cheerfully and willingly.

It isn't that you are likely ever to receive such treatment. It is very freeing, however, to be able to feel that you need *nothing* from anyone. Make God your only support and joy.

27. Overcome the natural need for self-importance by *enjoying* your own unimportance!

Years ago, I was invited to speak at a conference on communities. Several famous persons had been invited to speak. The convener had set up the conference to announce his plans for starting a community himself. I was, as it happened, the only person there who'd had actual experience in founding communities.

One evening during the week I invited several of the speakers out to dinner at a restaurant. For some reason, though we sat around the same table, they basically ignored me and spent the evening talking self-importantly to one another. The situation was especially unusual in that I was the host!

"This is beautiful!" I told myself. No one seemed interested in my opinions on anything. Therefore, while trying to be gracious, I said very little.

At first I was surprised to find how far I was in their minds from "center stage"; I played the part of an otherwise non-existent audience. I soon realized, however, that this was a golden opportunity to practice enjoying my own unimportance. I found the evening delightful, and relished the inner freedom I felt in that thought.

28. Every evening, as you review in your mind the events of the day, avoid the thought of

how *you* "stood up" in others' eyes: what kind of impression you made; the words you said; how you reacted; how others reacted to you. Instead, share with God any thoughts of this nature that come to you.

Be like Arjuna on the battlefield of Kurukshetra. His charioteer was Krishna, who took no active part in the struggle, yet by his very presence gave all the assurance Arjuna needed of ultimate victory.

Your thoughts, if you share with the Lord every recollection of the day, will soar above ego-consciousness.

29. An American swami from another ashram in India once visited me. After some discussion, he asked my advice on something that had been bothering him. "How," he wanted to know, "should I handle people's respect and reverence? In this country, swamis are treated as though all of them were saints. I know I shouldn't let it affect me, but what is the best way to overcome that temptation?"

After reflecting a little, I said to him, "Don't concentrate on what you are receiving from others: Concentrate on what you are giving out to them. Give them respect, even reverence, as children of God. Never forget that all human beings are equal, in Him."

30. How should you respond in the opposite situation, when others heap you with insults? In this case also, give back respect. Give back even reverence if you can universalize your feelings to that extent. After all, what is it that really matters? Truth! Is the insult justified? Then be inwardly grateful that someone did you the kindness of uttering it. Is it unjustified? Then wish to see the person or persons who insulted you released from that negative thought, which can only pull his or their consciousness downward.

Many years ago I encountered a man at a public function who had once been my friend, but who, since then, had turned against me. Smiling sincerely, I invited him to visit me some afternoon for tea. He responded, as he had often done, by excoriating me and Ananda. This person had accepted wholeheartedly the accusations my sister disciples made against me. I replied to his expressions of contempt by saying, "J——, I might be the Devil himself, but *even so* that wouldn't be *your* problem. Why let negativity rankle you? You are the one who is hurt by negative attitudes."

He shook himself as if to rid himself of mental cobwebs. "I know," he said. "I can't help it."

I felt sorry for him.

31. Some people find it helpful to tell funny or deprecating tales at their own expense—in a spirit of fun, not of heavy-hearted confession. This practice can be helpful, as long as it is engaged in with a measure of calm dignity. It may be helpful also to let people laugh at you, and helpful also to return their laughter in a spirit of fun.

    Delusion is extremely subtle, however. Don't indulge in such banter too long: One or two light exchanges should suffice. After that, turn the energy away again from yourself. For if, even in a spirit of fun, you draw energy and attention too much toward yourself, it will affirm your ego. The fruits of ego are green, because unripe, and are therefore sour. It is no accident that most comedians, in private life, are unhappy people.

32. Don't let your mind play with the thought of where and how you yourself fit into any picture. Don't toy with flattery by entertaining it even lightly in your mind. Reject sternly any thought of self-importance, self-praise, self-justification, and blame.

This subject is as important for you as your own salvation, for your spiritual liberation depends upon release from ego-consciousness.

If release from the prison of delusion is important to you, then everything I have written above is of supreme importance. It is a question of the direction you give your energy and consciousness. If you allow yourself to be affected, even minutely, by flattery, to that extent you will be affixing one more iron bar in the prison of your ego. And to the extent that you allow yourself to accept in your ego even the slightest energy, to that exact extent you will create more bondage for yourself.

Instead, therefore, seek in every way possible to expand your energy and consciousness *away from* yourself. In other words, don't expand your self-awareness like a balloon: *Release* it from all self-*definition*. Be quite stern with yourself in this practice, no matter how carefree you may seem in others' eyes.

33. These should be enough suggestions for now. The important thing is that any thought of yourself should be offered up instantly to God. Spiritual liberation comes not in one grand, overarching leap, but by

little increments of which the points I've suggested above will take you soaring.

Paramhansa Yogananda suggested that we memorize his poem, "Samadhi," and repeat it daily. In essence, he meant also that we should always dwell on the thought that our true reality is infinite. Make the state of omnipresence your constant affirmation.

(As I see what I've written above, I see that the thought might arise in some people's minds to print out these ideas in the form of my "secrets" booklets, with the suggestion to the reader that he practice one idea every day of the month. I am not in favor of that idea in the present context, however. These thoughts are not intended to be pondered in sequence, whether one of them a day throughout the month, or by any other system. It seems to me far better, instead, to practice them as often as the occasion arises.)

How to Be an Ego-Detective

Ego-consciousness is centered in the medulla oblongata at the base of the brain. Whenever you feel energy gathered in that spot, take it as an indication that your ego has been stimulated. Note this stimulation any time you feel flattered, or upset, or pleased with yourself, or (as I hope you never will be) arrogant.

When you feel any concentration of energy there, make a determined effort to relax at that point. Release the energy, and let it flow forward to the forehead at the point between the eyebrows, the *ajna chakra.*

VI

The Advantages of Formal Renunciation

Between worldly people and sincere renunciates the contrast is easy to discern. Worldly people, whether married or single, live primarily in the thought, "I . . . I . . . I," or, "mine . . . mine . . . mine!" True renunciates live for God, and try to conduct their lives by divine truth alone.

I won't go into the subjective aspects of this matter. Obviously, many apparently worldly people are not worldly at all, for in their hearts they live purely for God. And many so-called renunciates are arrogant, allowing their very act of renunciation to nourish their egos.

Let me therefore concentrate on the members of Ananda Sangha, and especially on the differences between those residents who have embraced formal renunciation and those who haven't. For every sincere Ananda member is, inwardly at least, a renunciate. Indeed, the only valid reason for joining an Ananda Sangha community is the desire to find God, and, as part of seeking Him, to serve Him in others.

Renunciation, then, for Ananda Sangha members means to renounce ego-identity above all. I have tried to make it clear that such renunciation is something everyone can embrace. Freedom from ego-involvement is easier to accomplish, however, if one also formally embraces the path of renunciation.

Why so? Because the way we define ourselves is, to a great extent, how others will define us. By formally renouncing worldly ties, a person makes a clear statement to this effect in his own mind. Formal renunciation makes it easier to project the consciousness of inner freedom to others. One finds it easier also to live by those standards if others know that he has firmly embraced a different set of values from their own, and from the norms of society. People will, for one thing, be less likely to try to engage him in worldly conversations.

Ease is, in fact, a primary issue. The path to God is not easy. Why, if one can help it, add unnecessary burdens to what one must carry anyway? Renunciation is like the familiar saying, "He travels fastest who travels alone." It may be said also, "He travels fastest who travels *lightly.*"

When one can make it clear to others that he is not personally interested in many things that interest most people, he will have fewer problems in dealing with them. Their expectations of him will be more in line with who and what he really is, and will spare both themselves and him unnecessary embarrassment. His family members, for instance, will be less inclined to expect him to be interested in all the things that fascinate them, but that might be in conflict with his renunciate calling. Members of the other sex will not be so inclined to risk rejection by trying to awaken his (or her) interest in them. Mothers of marriageable sons or daughters will more likely seek elsewhere for suitable mates for their children.

(I'm not going to go through the he/she thing any further. Please understand simply that "he," in this paper, as indeed in the English language, is both the masculine and the impersonal pronoun. When I say "he," then, my reference is to *both* sexes.)

A renunciate is armed with the perfect excuse for not involving himself in activities that are incompatible with his spiritual calling: visits to night clubs, for example, or going to dances. Without giving offense, he can plead off from attending weddings, baptisms, and other familial affairs that might be a contradiction to his chosen way of life.

Not all renunciates wear a formal monastic garb, but if one does so he should wear it with a loftier motive than to impress others. Indeed, he may not want to draw unnecessary attention to himself by wearing it. When traveling in public, for instance, he might be justified, even if he normally dresses as a monk, in wearing normal street clothing. The purpose of monastic dress is not outer display: It is a constant reminder to the renunciate himself of his sacred calling. It also makes it easier for others to know better how to relate to him. When others know, moreover, the kind of life to which he is dedicated, they find it easier to channel their communication with him toward worthy subjects.

A renunciate doesn't have to make the same effort worldly people must often make to please others. Often, those shallow courtesies are no more than oil, lubricating the machinery of social intercourse. The renunciate can show a certain eccentricity in these matters without giving offense, as long as he understands that the word "eccentric" means living centered in spiritual truth within, and doesn't mean looking upon others' opinions and attitudes as having a central reality.

A renunciate finds it easier to keep the motive of pleasing God and Guru uppermost in his heart. He needn't make unnecessary efforts to please people who don't share his spiritual outlook. Being unmarried, he has no need to respond to the superficial criticisms that husbands and wives often hurl at each other. (I'm reminded of a song that was fairly popular in America many years ago. A wife is nagging her husband: "Why don't you do right, like some other men do? Get outa here, and make me some money, too!") The renunciate has no need to justify himself before accusations like this, which have no spiritual validity. And he doesn't have to submit to the endless list of foolish expectations worldly people commonly hold of one another. It is enough, for him, to please God.

As for offspring, even spiritually dedicated couples might attract to themselves souls (egos, that is to say) that are burdened with heavy worldly karma. For the renunciate, there is simply no danger of this kind of imposition! (Indeed, the Bible's commandment to "be fruitful and multiply" is an invitation to a game something like roulette: How can anyone be sure into which slot the "ball" of fortune will fall? And who knows what entity will be drawn into his family, and thereby define it, to become for the rest of his life a responsibility—whether joyful or sorrowful.)

The renunciate need not adjust his wishes to, nor take personal responsibility for, children whose karmas are their own and may have nothing to do with his karma. He doesn't have to listen to worldly people urging him to "get ahead" in business or in anything else. He can forget other people's expectations of him, and not feel defensive when they criticize him. He can live centered and secure in himself, in his own values, his own system of beliefs, and his own devotion to truth and God.

VII

The Disadvantages of Formal Renunciation

There are disadvantages, also, to assuming the outward role of a renunciate. Perhaps the principal one is that, when one lives surrounded only by people who share his ideals, he may develop a condescending, or even a judgmental, attitude toward those whose ideals are different. He may steep himself thereby in ego-consciousness, instead of expanding from the little point of ego in himself to cosmic consciousness.

It is, in fact, a common disadvantage of formal renunciation that it tempts some renunciates to feel superior to worldly people. Thus, renunciation strengthens some people in their egos instead of helping them to dissolve their ego-consciousness. It is indeed more difficult, as Sri Ramakrishna said, to overcome spiritual pride than to lose worldly arrogance. Excessive satisfaction with one's own material or intellectual accomplishments, or with worldly position, soon meets its "come-uppance." As the waves on the ocean rise and fall, so on this ocean of delusion even the highest wave never remains high for long. Worldly exaltation is inevitably followed, sooner or later, by a crash of some kind—perhaps failure, perhaps scandal, perhaps defeat by enemies. Every outward success is succeeded by outward failure. Every joy is replaced by sorrow. Every fulfillment turns to disappointment.

Pride in one's own spiritual accomplishments, however, is based on something relatively real. The wave of spiritual pride may therefore take a long time—even incarnations—to subside. Be very careful, then, never to fall into this greatest of delusions.

I remember a period during my early days of discipleship when I was trying earnestly to conquer intellectual pride. I began after some time to feel that I was making significant gains in this attempt. Then one day, to my astonishment, I awoke to the realization that I was becoming proud of my humility!

Many swamis, I've observed, preen themselves foolishly on the respect they receive from other people. It pleases them to have people touch their feet or say to them (with no more meaning, usually, than if they'd said, "It's a nice day"), "Swamiji, everything will go well *provided that it has your blessings.*" Indeed, for many sannyasis this danger may far outweigh any benefits they might achieve by their formal renunciation.

My instinctive reaction when people in India touch my feet, which is their custom, is to feel that they are blessing me. The renunciate must never pride himself on his status in others' eyes. Nor should he feel that it entitles him to any increase of authority over others. Indeed, there seems to me something slightly comical in the big *mahant* proceeding grandly on the back of his elephant, protected by a flapping canopy!

Being served by others, instead of offering service humbly to them, may also make the renunciate not only proud, but selfish. He must make it an extra point to serve others as his Divine Friend, appearing to him in many forms. It is important that one show, and *feel* also, universal respect for even the ignorant. No matter how foolish another person may be, all men have this one point in common: the universal adventure all share of traveling together the path to ultimate enlightenment.

A further disadvantage to formal renunciation is that, because the renunciate is traditionally supposed not to mix with the other sex, his nature may develop one-sidedly, in either a masculine or a feminine way. Separation of the sexes, while desirable for renunciates, can in certain ways be unfortunate also. For the masculine and feminine natures are two halves of a whole. Neither is complete in itself.

As a man evolves spiritually, he acquires balancing feminine characteristics, developing a more feeling nature and becoming kinder and more compassionate. Even physically, there is a tendency to manifest feminine as well as masculine qualities:

His gestures become softer and more gentle, without becoming effeminate in the sense of conveying a hint of the message, "Look at me." His gaze, though direct, is also accepting of others and not challenging. Some men actually develop a suggestion of physical breasts.

On the other hand, as a woman evolves spiritually, her nature receives a balance of certain masculine traits. She becomes more impersonal, more impartial to all, and more inclined to balance her emotions with reason. Even physically speaking her walk becomes firmer; her gestures, more decided, less inviting. Her gaze, though loving, is not personal. (I observed all these traits in the great woman saint, Ananda Moyi Ma.)

Men saints frequently become more devotional: women saints, more impersonally wise.

Mixing only with members of one's own sex can be disadvantageous in the sense that one may not develop this balance. Men who lack an outer, softening feminine influence in their lives may become somewhat rigid and unsympathetic in their views and comportment. Women, on the other hand, may become over-reactive emotionally, prone to inconsequential gossip, and less generous-spirited, if people disagree with them.

Men tend more naturally to view nobility in terms of noble behavior. Women, on the other hand, tend to view it more in terms of high position. This may not be a fair assessment, but certainly it is true that men, generally, are more inclined to see things impersonally, and women, more personally.

A man once remarked to a woman friend of his, "Women take things too personally."

"Nonsense," the other snorted. "*I* don't!"

VIII

The Tally

What is wrong with this picture?—

The man is reasonable, fair-minded, and sincere; the woman is sweet, tender, and inspiring: the combination ought to work. Why does it so often not work at all?

For of course, it often fails miserably. Too seldom do men and women bring out the best in each other. And too often they bring out the worst. How can this be?

I have seen happy marriages in my life. Sometimes, to be sure, what looks like a happy marriage is simply acted out on the stage of society's opinion, to impress other people. In private, the swords of irritation, anger, and hatred are unsheathed.

Yogananda described a couple he'd met—ideally mated, so others believed—who, *behind* the scenes, quarreled viciously. In a different situation, on the other hand, where I myself lived "back stage" since it was in my own earthly home, I never heard a cross word pass between my father and mother. I cannot help believing that the same may be said of many homes. Why, then, have I described that marital harmony as an illusion? The sad truth is that even the best of marriages never fulfill the eternal longing of the soul. In this highest sense, dreams of human unity are sadly disillusioning. The love of man and woman, even at its best, is a compromise with the highest ideals, and cannot but disappoint the heart's natural yearning.

Last night (as I write these words), I and a small group of friends watched the Walt Disney animated movie, "Cinderella." I am no hard-hearted cynic when it comes to love: I *long* for it. It is *human* love that I see as the compromise, not divine love. As the movie ended with the lettered message, "And they lived happily ever after," I found tears in my eyes. "It's true!" I murmured. "That's just what happens for all of us!"

"You mean," someone said, "in *nirbikalpa samadhi*?"

"Of course," I replied.

The perfect love for which all of us long—that love which ends in absolute, unqualified bliss—awaits us in God. Nothing, outside of Him, will ever work.

When I met my Guru I said to him, "Marriage isn't for me."

"It isn't for anyone," he replied, and proceeded to tell me several stories of the disillusionments he had witnessed.

To develop an ideal balance between one's

masculine and feminine nature, one must develop inner communion with God. The degree of inner balance one achieves depends on one's degree of Self-realization. The Garden of Eden, so my Guru wrote, represented the inner bliss that man knew when he lived focused on the joy within, at the spiritual eye.

Paramhansa Yogananda added something quite strange: In Adam and Eve's communion at this point, they were actually able to produce physical offspring, inviting their souls down from the astral world.

"Offspring" can be taken also to mean spiritual inspirations and exalted creative works, which come when one's consciousness is uplifted. What the Bible means in stating that Adam and Eve were expelled from the garden of Eden is that their level of consciousness descended from the Christ center, becoming centered in the lower spinal centers.

The highest creativity results when the masculine and feminine energies are united in divine communion. As the energy descends in the spine, lower levels of creativity ensue, producing at last only physical progeny. To the degree that men and women find their unity on a lower level rather than in God, what they receive from each other is, to varying degrees, egoic in nature. In God alone lies perfection.

What, then, is the problem with human love? The answer is simple: human nature! Though everything is a manifestation of God, in separateness

from one another and from Him people take on littleness. A veil is cast over their consciousness.
Human beings become, consequently, darkened in
their understanding.

As human beings evolve, they perceive ever
more clearly the truth behind the veil of appearances. As long, however, as that truth is hidden
from them, they keep thinking, "I, I, I." Truth in its
highest aspect cannot but remain illusory.

The ego reaches outward through the senses to
the world around. Its soul-memory inspires it to
reach up toward perfect bliss. The spine is, both literally and symbolically, an expression of this truth.
That part of our consciousness which moves outward through the senses also moves downward in
the spine, creating at its base a south pole, which
opposes the north pole at the top of the spine.

When our self-awareness is centered between
the eyebrows, the harmony we feel with others is
spiritual in nature. The balance and harmony that
come when men and women mix together with
higher consciousness brings out in them the best
qualities. As their consciousness descends in the
spine, however, the quality of that interchange is
darkened, and the special attraction between them
strengthens their egos. The farther down in the spine
their consciousness is centered, the more keenly do
their egos desire to possess one another instead of
simply cooperating together in mutual harmony.

Of course, the more people's energy becomes

centered in the lower spinal centers, the more they feel drawn toward sexual expression. Originally, Yogananda said, Adam and Eve in the Garden of Eden attracted physical offspring by uniting their spiritual forces in the spiritual eye. People nowadays find it difficult even to visualize that process. When Eve was tempted by the serpent, what this meant was that she—representing the feeling aspect in human nature—recalled subconsciously the procreative process in the animal kingdom, and felt a degree of nostalgia for sexual expression.

Woman is traditionally viewed as the temptress. This is because the feminine nature represents the heart's feelings. On a practical level, of course, man also plays the tempter, and usually plays that role more aggressively. It is true nevertheless, however, that it is usually the woman who attracts, and the man who responds to the woman's subtle invitation. Because man's nature is outgoing, moreover, he often imposes himself where no invitation was extended.

The fact is, as energy becomes centered in the ego, it creates a vortex around the thought, "I . . . I . . . I . . . ." A magnetic field is thereby created. Between unenlightened men and women there exists an attractive power. To deny this reality, or to insist that it is all in the mind, would be foolish.

Most people cooperate with it gleefully. Nature pushes that cooperation along by making men and women physically attractive to each other, as well as attractive in their personalities and in their ways of looking at things, which often differ.

As for physical beauty, not only is it something that soon fades, but it is also the first attractive feature to lose its appeal, when people have been married even a short time. This doesn't mean that people come in time to see their beautiful partners as ugly. Rather, beauty in their partners simply becomes less interesting to them, being overshadowed by the personality's greater reality as it is more clearly revealed. For age is not the only thing that causes beauty to fade. Familiarity is another cause, once a personality ceases to be pleasing, and people realize how thoroughly appearances have duped them.

Again, let us ask our question: *What is wrong with this picture?* Sex seems exciting, wonderful, energizing, supremely enjoyable—GREAT! So why *shouldn't* men and women indulge in it to their hearts' content? Why not fairly soak themselves in it? The fact is, their hearts are *not* contented. The first and most obvious problem concerns the objective consequences: the squalling brood that, whether wanted or not, become a couple's responsibility. Much more, however, is involved in the problem.

The Hindu scriptures point out that sex increases the ego's grip on human nature. Women's eyes show increased pride. Men show not only a like increase, but also reveal a depletion of their mental energy. Sex takes more out of a man, for it is he who gives the energy. Women, however, in receiving that energy, reinforce their own sense of self-importance and self-worth. As Yogananda put it, in describing the attitude of many women in relating to their husbands: "There she sits like a queen, ruling him because he cannot rule himself!"

HM

Biologically speaking, the female function is to coax semen out of the male. Men who respond eagerly to this magnetism become what Yogananda called "sex wash-outs." Their energy for higher forms of creativity diminishes, and is drained at last of all power. Their will is weakened. Their magnetism for other creative activities is depleted. Both men and women become prematurely old, while the lines on their faces grow deeply etched. The expression in their eyes becomes, in time, tired and listless. Even their voices become brittle, as if needing lubrication; they seem to find it increasingly unpleasurable to speak. Their memory also becomes dulled.

With men, more is involved than tired energy. As the energy flows out from them with the expulsion of semen, their involvement in sexuality places a greater mental and spiritual drain on them. Yogananda said that every seminal ejection contains the equivalent, in energy loss, to a quart of blood. He said also, "For this reason, and because the sexual urge is stronger in men, the spiritual path is more difficult for men than for women." He added in consolation: "Those men, however, who get there become very great."

The power that is released for flowing upward in the spine of men who practice sexual self-control can bring them spiritual awakening. It is an enormous power.

There is a sect in Rumania of which the male members, after producing two or three children, undergo voluntary castration. Their purpose is spiritual, based—though invalidly—on the words of Jesus Christ: "There are eunuchs who made themselves eunuchs for the sake of the kingdom of heaven." (Matt. 19:12) Yogananda spoke strongly against this practice. The power generated in the testicles, he said, is extremely potent. Its purpose is to generate life. It can also empower a person's spiritual life, and, indeed, energize his entire consciousness. Lacking that power, the Master added, a man would become listless and low in energy, both spiritual and mental.

Having stated that the spiritual path is harder for men, Yogananda added, "Well, women have their problems too. They have greater attachment to *maya*." One need only see how women litter their shelves with pretty little nick-knacks to get something of what he meant. Notice also how advertisers, from experience, gear their copy more to women buyers.

One woman—my superior in the monastery many years ago—once remarked to me and another monk, "Let's face it, women are more spiritual than men." Nonsense! Men and women start out in the race of life on an even footing. Men in general have one set of obstacles; women, another. Victory is usually the greatest for those who have the greatest obstacles to overcome. Indeed, it is interesting to observe that the leaders in every field of life, including those in which women usually excel, are often men. As the Master put it, "When men get there, they become very great."

Sex is not an easy thing to dismiss from the mind, so long as the energy remains centered in the lower *chakras.* Sex ceases, however, to be a temptation when one's energy is centered higher in the spine. Sex has been described as the strongest instinct after self-preservation itself. The scriptures themselves exhort mankind to "be fruitful and multiply." Who would care to indulge in sex at all, however, were it not for the strong downward flow of energy that nature implants in all human beings, drawing their consciousness down in the body, and then outward?

The sex instinct can certainly be transmuted, but never by suppression. The temptation itself, therefore, if it comes, is nothing to be alarmed about. Neither is it something to occasion guilty feelings. The way to transcend sexual desire is by calm dispassion, not by violent rejection. If one seeks transcendence, he must practice dispassion by

56

calm non-attachment, while offering himself joy-fully up to God.

For most people, giving up sex seems possible only by suppression. Krishna says, however, in the Bhagavad Gita, "What can suppression avail?" ("Nothing," is what he implied.) The way of Nature is to procreate, but this is not the whole story of human existence. Creativity has higher octaves. Nature's ways can be manipulated by good sense. Self-control comes more easily to one who curbs his lower nature than to one who denies that he has lower urges. Marriage, for example, has the special advantage of limiting one to a single partner. This is a natural means for bringing sexual inclinations under control. The concept of platonic love is commonly misunder-stood. As it was conceived by Plato, he didn't mean that one should eliminate physical passion altogether. In fact, what he stated was that one should gradually reduce his physical desire to the point where two people can experience commun-ion together on a purely spiritual level.

After marriage—the desire for which many people find all-absorbing—people generally turn to other forms of creative outlet as well. With women, that outlet is, in most cases, their children and the creation of a beautiful home life. With men, their creative outlet is more often found in their work. Men may also develop hobbies that engross them—wood-working, for example. In time, these outlets for creative energy provide wholesome alternatives to sexuality.

It must be said, however, that all such activities strengthen the hold ego has on a person. It is only later in life that one begins to withdraw more or less naturally from outwardness, and to focus his sights on eternity.

The *"ashrams"* in ancient India were intended to lead those who felt so inclined through four natural stages of development, or "rest points," in their passage through life.

The first is *brahmacharya*, the student stage. Teenagers are urged to develop self-control on all levels, including above all the sexual.

Grihastha is second, the householder stage. During this period, it was anciently taught, one should seek fulfillment by performing his duties in the home and at work. The accumulation of wealth (*artha*) was considered a legitimate pursuit during this time of life, provided one did so *dharmically*, or ethically.

Vanaprastha, the third stage of life, is the time for serving others as a mature counselor. The *vanaprasthi* withdraws from excessive worldly concerns, but remains in the home sharing with others younger than himself what he has learned in life.

Sannyas or renunciation, finally, is the fourth stage, designed for those who, as they approach the end of life, want to focus their sights beyond this world on the time when they will have to leave this world for the next one.

In many cultures, particularly the American Indian, there used to be so-called "rites of passage" for that time when a boy enters adolescence. This would be an excellent concept for Ananda communities to embrace, for both boys and girls. I have hesitated thus far in Ananda Sangha's history to recommend this practice, out of concern lest I introduce it prematurely, and thereby do more harm than good. I didn't want the memory of failure to discourage its eventual adoption. Several Ananda members have occasionally seized on this concept to propose merely fanciful concepts for the community. If, now, after reading this paper, our members feel that the idea might be tried safely and not whimsically, then I am in favor of its adoption.

Is now the right time? Several people have, in fact, been recently recommending this concept to me, and I am more than open to adopting it. It is one I have toyed with in my mind for years. The important thing, I think, is that the concept be approached *with understanding.*

Let me explain what I think that understanding entails.

IX

Two Stages of Brahmacharya

I suggested earlier that renunciation is a difficult concept to instil in people, as long as society itself rejects certain norms that support the concept of self-abnegation. For modern society has gone off, instead, baying like a pack of hounds down the trail leading to self-gratification. Accepting the goal of life—rightly so—to be personal happiness, what people have done is look for shortcuts. And they've found them in abundance, in all the wrong ways!

The word "duty" has acquired a confused meaning. It could be equated, today, with those naughty four-letter Anglo-Saxon words one is taught to avoid in polite society. "I *want*" is the guiding concept in modern life. The natural brake to that concept, "I *should*," is greeted deprecatingly, as though self-control were a tiresome and old-fashioned notion.

In India, the ancient teaching on the four stages in life is virtually ignored these days. Young people attend school to learn how to earn a living, but are not taught how to live.

The *grihastha*, or householder, stage is generally

considered a time for enjoying sophisticated pleasures, along with working to maintain that kind of life, rather than working to fulfill one's social and spiritual duty.

The third stage, *vanaprastha*, is virtually ignored nowadays for the simple reason that what young adults learn has become passé by the time they've reached an age when they might have gained experience to pass along. People in their fifties and sixties must struggle to keep up with all the new information that is flooding the marketplace. They try to work as long into old age as possible, knowing that once they retire their days of usefulness will be over, and there will be nothing left to do but sit around, waiting to die.

The fourth stage, finally—*sannyas*—has become not at all what people still euphemistically call, "the golden years." The "Old folks," in their declining years, instead of devoting themselves to seeking truth and higher values have no role left to play in society, and nothing to which to aspire. Society is through with them. They, too, seem fairly well through with society. Between brief bursts of travel and gawking at the "sights," they throw their days away playing cards and watching television. Having been taught no worthwhile values in their childhood, all they know now is that life is ending with a gradual exhalation of physical weakness and, perhaps, senility.

Am I being perhaps too cynical? I cannot

forget my Guru once quoting *Adi* (the first) Swami Shankaracharya: "Childhood is busy with playthings; youth is busy with sex; young adulthood is busy with money and self-aggrandizement; old age is busy with sickness, worries, and fading memories. *No one* is busy with God!" The Master's comment was, "He was bitter, but, well, that is in fact how most people live." As Sri Krishna stated in the Bhagavad Gita, "Out of a thousand, one seeks Me."

How much more true is Shankara's statement today, when youngsters are taught that life has no noble purpose. Even people with inborn spiritual tendencies may end up thinking, "Oh, what's the use? One has to be reasonable. Maybe I'm crazy in wanting anything better than the normal, worldly grind." And those who succeed in preserving a sense of duty decide, very often, that their first responsibility is not to themselves and their own improvement, but to the world: to improve it somehow. How? By making it more comfortable, and life itself more convenient. How many people think of attuning their lives to God's will? Virtually none.

I am reminded of the woman who conceived the idea of Mother's Day. It was her lofty dream to enshrine motherhood as something holy and beautiful. How sad she became, decades later, to see her concept commercialized and degraded from her ideal. It had come to be celebrated by taking

"Mom" out to dinner at a fancy restaurant. And of course Mother's Day is a hot item in the greeting cards market.

Any attempt at improving the world that doesn't include improving the individual is almost sure to disappoint. The world is a school: not so much a thing to be improved, in itself, as an opportunity, giving people a chance to improve themselves.

It all begins with education. "As the twig bends, so doth the tree grow." In my book *Education for Life*, I explain that a human being needs four tools to become truly mature—a maturity which, I make clear, means more than becoming an adult. These tools are 1) physical coordination; 2) emotional control; 3) will power; and 4) intellectual clarity.

I associate these four stages with the first two cycles of Jupiter in a person's life. In Indian astrology, Jupiter is named "Guru." Its influence is to expand our understanding. One full cycle of Jupiter, or "Guru," requires twelve years to complete. During the first six years, this planet moves away from its birth placement in the chart; during the second six, it moves back to its point of origin. Thus, one phase of growth toward maturity is completed.

For the first six years of a child's life, its main preoccupation is with bringing its physical movements under control. This is a time when the child stumbles about, gradually learning muscular coordination. During these years, the child has very little control over its emotions. When a child weeps, it simply weeps; there isn't much that can be done about it.

Seven, more or less, is the age when appeals can be made to more in a child than its sense of fun. The next six years are a time when it can be inspired by noble sentiments and ideals.

At thirteen, more or less, the child reaches puberty. For many children, this is a time of rebellion, meaning simply that they feel a need to test their will power—to "flex their muscles," so to speak, or "spread their wings" preparatory to flying by their own power.

At nineteen—again, more or less—the child begins to think more seriously for himself, to exercise and develop his intellect preparatory to deciding on the future directions he will take in life.

As I've pointed out, these stages cannot be demarcated absolutely. Some children are precocious, and in different ways. The general *direction* of development, however, is what I have stated. Children are deprived of the necessary all-rounded development if their elders try to "force feed" them prematurely—for example, by cramming their heads with advanced knowledge while the children are still very young.

To return to our basic subject, in the ancient Hindu system proper education required a stage of *brahmacharya*, which began with puberty at the age of twelve or thirteen. The word means, literally, "flowing with Brahma." Just as a surfer must learn the proper muscular control for flowing with the waves, so a human being needs to learn self-control—morally, emotionally, and intellectually—before he can attune himself to, and "flow" with, truth.

The stage known as *brahmacharya* bears the same name as the first stage of renunciation. In both cases, the name means self-control on every level. The usual connotation of *brahmacharya* is sexual self-control, but that is because sex is, of all instincts, the most difficult to control. Without some measure of such control, moreover, one's whole life will move like a runaway train, ready to jump its tracks at any moment.

Brahmacharya is greatly assisted, for adults, if they have received training for it during adolescence.

Early childhood, before sexual awakening, is a sweet period of life, usually unburdened with worries and responsibilities. When a child arrives at adolescence, sexual desire begins to awaken in it. It is important during this period that children begin to assume responsibility for their behavior. When they reach adulthood, they must be ready to play a serious role in society.

To review briefly the four stages of responsibility (leaving out, that is to say, the more-or-less irresponsible years of infancy and early childhood), one proceeds from adulthood to semi-retirement— a time for gradually handing the reins over to one's successors; then, finally, comes old age, which is, ideally speaking, a time for thinking of God and spiritual values.

I have always, for some reason, been particularly struck by the change in the sound a male calf makes, first as a calf, and then after it becomes a bull. Its relatively impotent bleat becomes a deep, aggressive bellow. Of course, human beings' voices change too, especially men's, but it is the aggressiveness of that bovine bellow that has especially impressed me. It suggests the sudden appearance within the animal of a new sense of self-importance and self-confidence. This awareness coincides with the dawn of sexual maturity. Is this not true of human beings, also?

X

A Suggested Rite of Passage

Many societies have so-called "rites of passage" for significant changes in a person's social status: manhood, for example, and marriage. The American Indians celebrated the passage out of boyhood. I am only minimally acquainted with their practices: with dream quests, and the rest. In any case, we live today in different times, and cannot merely imitate what has been done before. Today's emphasis, moreover, should be on training girls also for adulthood, and not only boys.

I have long thought it would be good for Ananda Sangha communities, and perhaps, someday, for society as a whole, inspired by Ananda's example, to develop some special ritual as a means of honoring the child's transition from childhood to sexual maturity. It has astonished me, in fact, that society demonstrates so little concern for this highly significant event. Certainly it is an occurrence of the highest importance in everyone's life. Perhaps the reason it is not given more attention is, first, that children become sexually mature at different ages, and, second, that the subject is too embarrassing for most adults, especially parents, to discuss with children.

Obviously, there is a need for the facts of life to be taught, impersonally. I myself don't think, however, that the best place to teach them is the classroom. It seems to me it would be a good thing for society itself to take on this responsibility. For sex should be taught as more meaningful than a merely biological act. There are deep—indeed, spiritual—aspects to the sex drive. The spiritual side of this subject is, unfortunately, little known these days. For many reasons, however, and by no means only spiritual ones, this is a subject people tend to sweep figuratively "under the carpet."

Most growing children, surely, are dismayed when they first learn how they were conceived. Their parents, quite understandably, are reluctant to tell them, since the children will almost certainly begin thinking, "You mean . . . you . . . *you* . . . ? Oh, *no!*" The information, for them, is traumatic.

And then the youngsters' own bodies begin to behave strangely, often causing them considerable shame.

The nature of any "rite of passage" into adolescence is not a matter for deep exploration here, since our subject concerns renunciation for grown adults. The essence of what needs to be emphasized for children, however, is the same as for those who, later on, become renunciates. And it is important for every human being to realize that sex was given us for a serious purpose, and not for free and undisciplined indulgence. Those who are not initiated early into these mysteries, as they truly deserve to be called, will have to learn them "in the streets," so to speak, later on in life by personal and perhaps ignoble experience when, for most of them, it will be too late to benefit from the opportunity for proper training.

I suggest for any rite of passage that an age be selected *before* puberty—perhaps the age of ten. It should be, in other words, a time of preparation for what is to come. Emphasis should be placed on the third stage of maturity, when the will needs to be developed discriminatingly. Particular emphasis should be given to the need for developing will power through sexual self-control.

Children should be taught that they have within them a sleeping dragon—known in the yoga teachings as the *Kundalini* power—which can grant powers of great accomplishment, or which can, on the other hand, reduce them to weak reeds, leaning for support on their stronger fellows for whatever advancement they get in life.

Delusion, like the serpent in the Garden of Eden, is extremely subtle. Something which girls and boys soon discover is their power to attract, and also influence, each other. Soon, they begin to identify power itself with the influence they can exert over the opposite sex. The song, "It Ain't Necessarily So," from *Porgy and Bess* states scoffingly, "Methuselah lived nine hundred years. . . . But who'd call that livin', when no gal will give in? To Methuselah, what's nine hundred years?" Such is the lie which Satan insinuates into the minds of the young.

Any rite of passage offered to children as they approach adolescence should emphasize the fragility of this particular kind of "power." Life should be explained to them as a long-distance run for which they must prepare carefully. The subject of sexual self-control is delicate, and may well not be easy to discuss. Adults should not flinch, however, from explaining what happens when people live wrongly. It will help their explanation if they use examples (not too personal) that the children will recognize.

It is very difficult for a child to imagine itself old. It may help to tell him that his present stage of life is one he has known before, and that old age, too, will all too soon be with him again. The speed with which life passes should be emphasized in every "rite of passage."

A little girl once asked me, "How old are you?" (I think I was nearing seventy at the time.) I answered her, "Let me put it this way: When I was your age, you were an old woman." Young people should be helped to understand that they, *themselves*, will someday be grown-ups, then old, and then—finished!

Boys should be helped to understand that the power they exert over girls is a trap in which they themselves may someday be caught! (Consider the large number of silent husbands in the world. Their wives do almost all the talking, and make most of the decisions!)

Girls should be shown that the power they exert over boys—a fact which they find delightful, after an early childhood of being pushed aside or ignored by boys—brings resentment in the male, resulting in the well-known "war of the sexes." The masculine advantage of having larger muscles is well compensated for by the feminine sharp tongue. Youthful feminine triumph yields, however, ere long, to the disappointment and pettiness of a complaining and unfulfilled existence.

Indeed, the ego cannot possibly fulfill even the least of its promises—if only because it is, itself, so disappointingly minute! Sex, which seems at first to promise a joyful, indeed a glorious existence, shows itself at last to be the Great Liar, its flowers strewn on gale winds as the "little ones" produced by sex all too often disappoint their parents' hopes. Life itself is a gray compromise. Each generation behaves as if it had at last discovered the wonders of sex! And each generation soon finds itself trudging wearily along a winding road, hemmed in on both sides by barren fields of disappointment.

None of this is to say that human love cannot be beautiful, ennobling, and even inspiring. Even at its best, however, it is something experienced still by the ego, and therefore drastically limited.

Human love is short lived, moreover: it is like brief rainfall on dry land. If life finally disappoints people, it is because man was not made for this world, but for communion with God. Our confinement in an ego is forever disillusioning. Even the noblest and most beautiful human love is like a sliver of glass, shining with reflected light from God's love.

Why is it that so many people are fooled? Because they delude themselves thinking, "The majority *can't possibly* be wrong!" The plain truth is quite the opposite: The majority is almost *always* wrong!

Sex should be described to children as an expression also of love, not of lust, and not as a merely scientific fact, which to children may seem even bestial and unclean. If connecting sex with love seems strange to children before sexual feeling stirs within them, it may help to explain to them that when there is deep love between husband and wife there is sometimes a desire even for complete physical union, rather resembling the way children like to be held and caressed. Between parents, it may be explained, there is a special relationship that is holy, and one that isn't shared with anyone else, as well as one which is too adult for children to understand.

Sex is a wonderful force, when it is understood and used rightly. It contains the secret of life itself. When that secret is explored at its source in deep spiritual feeling, it contains the key to the very mystery of our existence. Children who can be made to understand and appreciate this truth will be able to develop in themselves the magnetism to attract suitable mates, to attract popularity and success in life, and to retain youthful energy late into old age. Those, on the other hand, who abuse this power become, as Yogananda put it, "sex wash-outs" even while they are still in their youth.

I propose a ritual in which several older men—five might be a good number—address a group of ten-year-old boys, and in which a comparable number of women address a group of ten-year-old girls. It would be good to make this a solemn occasion. There could be a fire ceremony, accompanied by chanting (the *Mahamritunjaya* mantra comes to mind); a special blessing; a devotional chant to God, a prayer, and a short meditation. Each child could be given an Ananda pin to wear made of silver, with a small zircon or similar bright stone centered within the arrowhead.

I do not propose here to go more deeply into the subject of training the young. *Brahmacharya* is a vitally important stage of life, but since it usually leads to marriage, not to renunciation, I will limit this discussion to those who want to become life-long *brahmacharis*. This paper is for those who embrace formal renunciation. It is also for those who are married, even if they have children, who have realized that the true purpose of life is to find

God. Thus, couples, too, can follow these principles, at least inwardly.

This paper is above all for those unmarried persons who want to give their lives to God. Formal renunciation may help to protect them against the temptation, whether inwardly or from others, to seek companionship in human intimacy rather than in God alone.

How are people to avoid the trap of emotional attachment? Young people, especially, should not take lightly the drawback of false expectations. Emotional attachments lift people on high waves, which cannot but crash in the end. The desire for human affection is all but universal. Many people don't even see sexual desire as self-weakening: To them it is a simple fact, and even a blessing—perhaps a source, not of weakness, but of strength.

XI

The Second Brahmacharya

We come now to *brahmacharya* with special
emphasis on its more usual connotation of sexual
self-control. It is important to understand that the
attraction of the sexes for each other is not merely
"in the mind." It is a magnetic force to which
everyone, regardless of age, is sensitive. This fact is
evident, for example, in the special tenderness old
people often demonstrate toward the young, especially of the opposite sex. Yogananda said to me,
"The attraction exists at every age." A relative of
mine once, speaking of her three-year-old daugh-
ter, told me, "She has a special giggle that she
reserves just for little boys her age."

The attraction between the sexes need not be
physical. It depends on where a person's consciousness is centered in the spine. If one has the slightest
feeling that people of the other sex are somehow
special, he should recognize that feeling as a warning sign in himself.

One of the principles for *brahmacharis* always
to practice, under every circumstance, is to *internalize* every slight feeling of attraction. This is true,

indeed, of all kinds of attraction and is not limited to one's feelings for the opposite sex. It may be a simple liking for a piece of beautiful music, or a painting. Whatever pleasure you feel in anything, *internalize it*. Recognize that the source of that enjoyment is within yourself, in *your own reaction*.

Consider the example of little children at the zoo. How enthusiastic they are as they behold all those exotic animals! Their fascination dwindles, however, as they become fatigued. It isn't that the experience ceases to interest them. What diminishes is their ability to appreciate it, for their level of energy has decreased. By the end of the day, they want nothing more than to return home. They've learned, perhaps for the first time, that pleasure lies not in things, but *in one's ability to respond* to sense stimuli.

Thus, whenever you see a beautiful scene, for example, be aware of that inner lift of pleasure— perhaps even of happiness—within yourself, and then uplift that feeling to God. Share your heart's feelings with Him.

When you hear a beautiful sound—music, or the soothing sound of wind in the trees or of ocean surf on a beach—bring the consciousness of God into your appreciation of that beauty. In fact, in certain sounds of this world there is a suggestion of the sound of *Aum*, the creative vibration of the universe. Share your experience of everything with *Aum* as God, and rejoice with Him.

Train yourself never to enjoy anything *avidly.*
(The exaggerated glee and delight displayed in television commercials is a good example of what I
mean by "avidly.") Don't pour energy out through
the senses toward anything. Internalize whatever
sense-stimulation you experience, and remind
yourself that the very power to *enjoy* that experience lies within yourself, not in anything external.

Thus, look . . . briefly appreciate . . . and then
turn within or look away from the object that
engaged your interest. Give thanks to the Creator
for every worthwhile experience in life.

XII

Specific Suggestions for the Practice of Brahmacharya

Here are a few rules or, rather, helpful suggestions:

1. Make it a special point not to let persons of the other sex engage your attention too closely. Don't feast your gaze on them, whether or not you consider them pleasing to look at. (They will in any case have a certain magnetism.) Don't make a big thing of *not* looking at them: For example, don't drop your gaze hastily to the ground or the floor, or look hurriedly away as if startled or afraid. (There is no surer clue to your susceptibility to another person, or hint of dread, than hasty withdrawal. Some people will take their very suspicion of weakness in you as a challenge to try to make a new "conquest.") Instead, therefore, simply look away, impersonally.

2. The first thought of sex, even if it comes without a suggestion of attraction, is the moment to beware. Catch that thought, and redirect it elsewhere. Never tell yourself, "Oh, there's no harm in *thinking*!" There is, in fact, *every* harm! The factory of the mind is where temptation is first created.

3. When people of the other sex give the slightest indication that they find you attractive, don't try to analyze your own feelings in the matter. (You might decide that they have a point!) Instead, immediately impersonalize those feelings. I found when I was a young man, even before I met my Guru, that this simple response often sufficed to get a woman to leave me strictly alone. When she saw my impersonality, she decided I wasn't a "good catch."

4. For my part, in those days, the more likely it seemed that I might feel attracted to some woman, the more I instinctively put up a shield of impersonality. It worked: Girls generally turned away to seek elsewhere.

5. Another trick I found useful was to talk abstract philosophy at them! Doing so dampened effectively any interest they

might have had, especially when I indicated a lack of interest in persuading them to my ideas.

6. Discourage the thought in yourself, "She's a woman," or, "He's a man." Train your mind to look upon others simply as human beings.

7. Strangers on the street or elsewhere can exert a passing fascination also: Don't let your gaze linger on them. It may be enough simply to look away, but I suggest also making a point of *withdrawing your energy* from that scene, lest there linger some thought in the mind that you may have to deal with, later on.

Try not even to notice them. Remember, even if most people of the other sex awaken no interest in you, you may be surprised someday to find that *one face* particularly, one pair of eyes, lingers in your mind and becomes increasingly difficult to dismiss.

8. Try not to look lingeringly even at photographs of people of the other sex, especially if you find them attractive. Advertisements, particularly, are of course *designed* to attract. Pull in your psychic antennae, every

time you find yourself confronted by a barrage.

9. The human voice can have powerful magnetism. Use your own voice consciously to send out vibrations of harmony, peace, and inspiration. Take pains not to use your voice to attract others to yourself. And when you feel magnetically drawn to anyone by his voice, be especially attentive. You can't close your ears to the sound, but you *can* withhold your energy from it. Tell yourself, "All beauty comes from God."

10. Touch is the principle channel of sexual magnetism. Try to avoid all physical contact with the opposite sex. The dignified palms-folded *namaskar* used in India is better always than shaking hands.

Hand shaking, Yogananda said, creates a special, magnetic interchange, forming two "horseshoe" magnets. One is of the upper body; the other, of the lower body. In every interchange of magnetism, the Master made a strong point of explaining, the stronger magnet, either good or evil, will always affect the weaker.

11. Avoid the practice—increasingly common

nowadays—of embracing others, even of your own sex. A hug may be intended only to display affection and friendship; nevertheless, it is better to express those feelings in a higher way.

I myself developed a distaste for this practice when I realized how often people embrace one another, not with sincere feeling, but simply out of social habit. Usually, the gesture is quite meaningless. I feel much more love and friendship in my heart by not gripping others in a "bear hug"—an awkward gesture, at best! Thus, my practice is not to hug anybody.

12. Avoid the company of worldly people as much as possible. Don't be rude, of course, but don't show particular interest in the things that engage them.

13. Dress neatly and tastefully. Otherwise, however, don't be excessively careful of your appearance, especially not to look *attractive.* This suggestion is particularly important for women.

My Guru once said to his women renunciate disciples, "Ladies, don't pay too much attention to your appearance, lest you fall into temptation."

14. If persons of the opposite sex, especially, pay you compliments, watch your heart's feelings and ward off any special pleasure you might feel in either their words or their attitude. Don't reject their compliments, since to do so might seem rude. Rather, simply tell yourself, and the other person also (if tact and graciousness permit it) that everything praiseworthy comes from God.

15. If anyone's beauty strikes you, imagine that person sixty years from now. Life passes so quickly! Whatever a person's present age, he should never be defined by that.

16. Attraction often flourishes in the soil of merriment. Never allow your amusement in mixed company to cross the line into hilarity. Be friendly, be even humorous, and smile easily, but also maintain always, especially in mixed company, a certain calmness and dignity.

17. Because sexual attraction can arise in one when he is alone also, remember again Yogananda's advice: "The first thought of sex is the moment to catch it. Put that mere thought out of your mind; then direct energy into thinking about something else."

That first thought may be quite casual, and

may have no energy behind it. Even so, it is better to turn away from it.

18. When you feel the slightest stir of temptation inwardly, inhale and exhale deeply several times. This will make a magnet of your lungs. Draw the energy upward. Then sit in meditation, and focus your mind in the spiritual eye; be conscious of the magnetism there. Direct your entire energy-flow upward to that point.

19. Affirm frequently in yourself, "I belong to no one, and no one belongs to me. I need no one; no one needs me. I am complete in myself."

20. Keep in mind these words which my Guru once addressed to me: "Remember, you won't be safe until you reach *nirbikalpa samadhi.*"

Paramhansa Yogananda once told me, "Sri Ramakrishna had a young male disciple of whom he used sometimes to say, 'He was born, and I was born.' The statement led some people to conjecture, 'Who came because of whom?'

"One day this disciple told Ramakrishna

that he was meditating with a young woman.

"*Sadhu*, beware!' said the Master. [A sadhu is a holy man. A *brahmachari* is one who aspires to holiness.]

"'Oh, I will be all right,' said the young man. Well, after some time he 'ran away' with the woman. Remember, sadhu: Beware!"

XIII

How to Be a Temptation Detective

The point from which energy leaves the spine and goes out to the sex nerves is called the *swadisthan chakra*, or sacral center, located about an inch and a half up from the base of the spine. Sexual stimulation brings with it a sort of "thrill" of energy at that point. Whatever your mind tells you, if you have any sensation there, be very wary.

Another sensation also signifies an invasion of temptation: a stimulation of energy in the sex nerves themselves.

When you notice a stir in either location, uplift the energy through the spine to the brain by inhaling and exhaling deeply several times; then sit, and focus your energy deeply at the point between the eyebrows. The feeling of stimulation, however slight, is a warning sign that you should take extra care over the way you are directing your thoughts and energy.

Deep breathing, followed by meditation, is especially helpful. A sensation of coolness in the sex nerves will be spiritually helpful. You can generate this sensation artificially by touching something cool or even cold to that area. Feel the coolness rise up the spine to the brain, cooling it.

XIV

Poverty vs. Simplicity

There is a story told in India about a sadhu who went to the local police to report a theft.

"What have you lost?" demanded the officer in charge.

"Well, I've lost my home, my bedding, my table, my chair, my overcoat—in fact, I've lost everything!"

The police officer pondered a moment. "I don't understand," he said. "Aren't you living alone on a hillside?"

"That's true," acknowledged the sadhu.

"Then how could you have . . . ? Oh, never mind. Would you please describe for me what you lost?"

"Yes. It was a large, square piece of cloth about so big." The sadhu extended his arms upward and downward, then out to his side. For him, that one cloth had been serving all those functions.

Non-possession, for the renunciate, is an important principle. Certain Roman Catholic convents encourage their nuns in the thought of non-possession by having them say, "our," instead of, "my"—thus: "I am returning to our cell [where she sleeps alone]," or, "In the morning, the first thing I do is don our habit [monastic dress]."

My Guru did not emphasize poverty as a necessity for his renunciate disciples. The word he recommended was *simplicity*. I've found in my own experience that people who own nothing at all, or virtually nothing, must live very much at their own center. Otherwise, complete non-possession may negatively affect their natural dignity. The case varies with individuals, of course, but complete non-possession works best for hermits who can immerse themselves solely in the thought of God. Most renunciates are apprentices in that practice. If their natures are affirmative, they may accept non-possession cheerfully, but for most people the practice of owning nothing can lead to feelings of oppression. If people haven't the freedom to decide *anything* for themselves, the monk who receives no spending money of his own is likely to be like a plant in a deep forest, becoming spindly as it reaches up toward the sun. Though ascetic in appearance, perhaps, such a monk's feelings may be starved quite unnecessarily for those little fulfillments which might help him to be relaxed and more natural in his spiritual search. He may find the custom of complete non-possession more suppressive than liberating.

I can somehow believe more easily in the raven that brought St. Paul his daily loaf of bread in the desert than in the impartial charity of monastic superiors whose duty is to supply their subordinates' needs.

Some people reach liberation by expanding their self-awareness to infinity. Others achieve it by reducing the thought of self to non-existence. Both attitudes are expansive and beautiful. The mistake superiors often make, however, is to try to force everyone into the same mold. Indifference to individual needs, and even to people's special realities, does more harm than good.

St. Francis of Assisi is fondly remembered for his love affair with "Lady Poverty." Yogananda, who described Francis as his "patron saint," said also, "Instead of 'Lady Poverty,' I prefer the expression, 'Lady Simplicity.'"

"Money," you may have heard it said, "is the root of all evil." The saying is quite wrong, of course. The root of all evil, insofar as it concerns money, is the *desire* for money—or, as St. Paul of Tarsus put it, "*love* of money." An alternative to this definition might be, "*Attachment* to money is the root of all evil." At any rate, no mere *thing* is ever evil. It is what people *do* with things that is good or bad. In fact, some people do a great deal of good with their money.

Money and possessions, like every delusion, are harmful principally in strengthening ego-consciousness. In traditional monasteries, the practice of having no personal money is of course intended to free members from attachment to money.

I wonder to what extent, however, complete lack of money doesn't in some way, at least, inhibit a person's creativity. It is very well not to care about wealth, but not to care how one's needs are met also suggests to my mind a kind of passivity that cannot, in itself, lead to God-realization. When your superiors, out of a wish to encourage you to depend completely on God, provide you with every need, the chances are you will find yourself depending on them rather than on God. Monasteries generally approve of this spirit of passive dependence. I cannot say, however, that I have ever seen anyone particularly benefited by this attitude.

What I think such passivity usually develops, rather, is a kind of *sudra* attitude—a weakness of will that diminishes one's courage and ability to stand firmly on his own feet in the face of everything. Any self-debasing attitude cannot but be spiritually harmful.

As with humility, non-possession should be practiced intelligently, not mindlessly. Not to care at all where money comes from, how it is used, or how it *might* be used can in some cases be admirable, but I think it usually argues a lack of interest in one's surroundings that suggests, not perfect surrender, but only dullness of mind.

To be completely dependent on God's bounty is wonderful, provided one's attitude of dependence is active and positive, and entails constant, joyful self-offering to the Lord. Otherwise, one can gain little from letting others make all one's decisions for him.

A superior in the monastery I lived in once said to me, "In a corporation [she was thinking, of course, of monastic "corporations"], no one has a right *even to think* except the members of the board of directors." I was myself, at the time, on the board of directors; otherwise I'm sure she would not have dared to utter those words to me. Yet, even as a director I found that I wasn't really given much freedom to think.

Having no money at all in a monastic community makes the monks too dependent on others. Even if a monk has no desire for money, and finds it freeing not to think about it, his position of having to ask for everything he needs can be demeaning.

I once faced some of this problem myself. It was many years ago, and I was new at Mt. Washington (the headquarters of my Guru's organization). My repeated requests for curtains, which were needed in my room, produced no results. I was a new member, and quite young. Perhaps my requirements were not considered important. Months passed, at any rate, and no curtains arrived.

The building I lived in was a little two-room affair in the garden several yards from the main building. This small cottage had once served as a waiting room for cable cars that came up the hill from Marmion Way. The windows of my residence were exposed, obliging me, every time I dressed or undressed, to turn off the one light that dangled from the ceiling. Otherwise, I would have been seen by anyone passing by.

One evening I rebelled. Stripping down to my undershorts, I lay face down on the bed and gave myself up to the luxury of reading Shakespeare. Some little while later one of the senior nuns passed my window on her way back from the garage. Paying no attention, I went on with my reading— smiling to myself, however, at the probable consequences of my little "rebellion."

The following morning I received word that I would be getting my curtains.

An amusing incident, perhaps, though it suggests that I didn't belong to the "passive class" of renunciates. I tell the story here to illustrate the fact that monastic poverty, though in some ways a noble ideal, can also produce problems if one is obliged to depend wholly on the will of others.

Depending on God alone for everything is spiritually strengthening. The effect is lessened, however, when one has to depend on specific leaders in a community—even if they themselves are dedicated to God. The gains from letting others fulfill all one's needs cannot equal the gains derived from self-effort.

Strange, perhaps, to relate, politics often enter into a community when money is over-controlled. Favoritism and inequality rise to the surface. Some people begin to try to please their superiors. Thus, cliques develop.

I have always had the grace of being able to

attract to myself whatever I've needed in life. When I've found it necessary to depend on others to fulfill those needs, however, I have not been so successful. Surely it is good to affirm, *in a spirit of inner freedom*, one's ability to live happily with whatever God gives one. To have to rely on the charity of others, however, is, I think, a way of muddying the stream of grace. What one really affirms, in that case, is dependence on *others'* attunement with God's will.

I consider my Guru's solution the best. He arranged that we each receive a small allowance, rendering it unnecessary for us to submit a request for our every need. It was good for us, he felt, to do some things for ourselves. He never insisted, moreover, that we turn over to the organization all our possessions, or any funds that came to us from relatives or others. Thus, in my own case, I was able to do a number of things that were meaningful for me, and also gave money generously from time to time to the work.

One time, however, my father sent me $500 worth of Gulf Oil stocks. SRF's president insisted—this was years after our Guru's passing—that I give those stocks to the organization. I did so out of obedience, but I never felt comfortable about having done so, because I'd responded to her insistence and not acted of my own free will. It wasn't that I was attached to my father's gift. As one whose responsibility was helping to develop our monastic way of life, however, it seemed to me this was a wrong direction to take. It would have been spiritually better for me, I felt—and still do feel—to be generous on my own initiative than because of some rule.

Years later, after my separation from SRF, this was the only thing that I asked be returned to me. Everything else had been my free gift to my Guru, and I never wanted it back. This one thing, however, seemed to me a different case.

Monastic rules used, in the past, to be written with a view to ensuring the monastics' holiness. This was a medieval way of thinking. When organizing the SRF monks, I read the rule of St. Teresa of Avila, and was forcibly impressed with the thought that imposing rules to make people holy was no longer a good idea. No one can be *made* holy. I soon realized that it was time for a new kind of monasticism. Yogananda himself hadn't been able to devote much time and energy to this project, having had a much larger mission to initiate. At this time, however, he told me, "Don't make too many rules. It destroys the spirit." In organizing the monks, I kept a mind-set of careful attunement with him, and often sought his verbal counsel and approval.

It soon became apparent to me that any rule I instituted would be a compromise for those who were sincere. Several of the monks had been accustomed to meditating long hours. With a rule-mandated schedule, however, group meditation would oblige the sincere ones to meditate less. On the

other hand, no rule would make the lighter ones
more dedicated to a meditative way of life. Any
rule would be—would *have* to be—a compromise
in mediocrity. Better this compromise, however,
than a community that wasted too much time in
light-minded chatter. Our Guru wanted us to meditate as a group. No one previously in charge of the
monks had been willing to court unpopularity by
imposing such a system. Classes and meditations
were more or less left to individual preference.

I decided we must have some kind of system.
Too many of the young men, habituated formerly
to living as they pleased, were forsaking the monastic way of life. I decided to curtail my own meditations voluntarily, in order to ensure that everyone
meditated regularly.

For me this was, as I said, a compromise. I realized from the start, however—and my Guru con-
firmed it—that no one could be made holy by any
rule. Our spiritual perfection was *his* job, but he
pointed the way for me by never *forcing* his will on
anyone. The best I could hope for, then, was to keep
the monks from disturbing too much the over-all
calmness. I was gratified to see, after the new system
was instituted, that fewer of the monks left.

Since then, I have seen many monasteries. In
1963 I even lived for six months in a Roman
Catholic monastery, months after my separation
from SRF. I have become convinced that spiritual
development cannot be brought about by outward

measures. Rules can only prevent people from falling below a certain level of mediocrity. Otherwise, every individual must develop his own attunement with God. As our Guru put it, "You must individually make love to God."

To return to the subject of money, then: I think it is important not to enforce non-attachment by rule. Wealth should not be encouraged, of course, but I have seen that when people are *encouraged* to be non-attached of their own free will, rather than deprived of money systematically, they are much more likely to practice this virtue sincerely.

My Guru agreed with common spiritual tradition in considering money to be one of three great delusions—the other two being sex and "wine," or intoxicants of all kinds. Money strengthens ego-identification by increasing one's sense of power and importance. If a person wants to know God, he must shun values that worldly people consider normal. Their desires and ambitions are centered in the ego. To transcend ego-consciousness, one must consider everything as belonging to God.

The reason for the scriptural warning against the "three great delusions" is that they are the chief causes of ego-bondage. Where money is concerned also, ego, and not wealth as such, is the issue. Renunciates may be as proud of having no possessions as any merchant may be of his wealth. The particular delusion of money is that it suggests innumerable possibilities to the mind, and not only one attraction at a

time. When one's dreams focus on the source of ɛ
ply rather than on any specific thing, he may imagine
even building a castle with the thousand dollars in his
pocket. It is only when he takes seriously into
account just what is required to build such a structure
that he modifies his dream. In vagueness, one is more
easily caught in a trap of restless desires.

It may be better to allow the water contained by
a dam to flow out slightly than to keep that structure
under constant, maximum pressure. Letting the
renunciate have a little spending money not only
helps him to have a greater sense of independence—
which monastic tradition deplores, but which
Yogananda considered desirable—but will help his
spiritual development, which requires *self*-effort.

Worldly desires always cause energy to flow
out from the heart toward the objects of attraction.
Watch the flow of your heart's energy. Keep that
flow reined in, especially when money is concerned, affirming, "I am complete in myself."

It is an interesting fact that when the desire for
money is brought under control; when money
ceases to exert a fascination; when one has schooled
himself to think of wealth only in terms of the good
it can do: then he attracts money almost effortless-
ly, in any amount that he needs.

Try to practice regularly the following techniques for overcoming attachment to money:

XV

Techniques for Dealing with Money

1. Whatever money you receive, place it mentally (or literally) on an altar as an offering to God. Pray that it serve a good cause.

2. Give to God, or to some good cause in His name, a portion of whatever money comes to you.

3. On your birthday—which tradition marks as a day when you receive presents—make gifts to your friends as an expression of gratitude for God's countless gifts to you— including, above all, the gift of life itself.

4. If you suffer pain or sorrow of any kind, look for someone less fortunate than yourself, and help him. Offer him, if you think it will help him, a monetary gift.

5. When giving gifts to others, try to give also the gift of happiness. Give not only something you think they may want, but something

you'd feel happy in giving them. Material gifts are mere things, but the wishes for others' happiness that you infuse into those things are the *real* present you give them.

6. When buying something, don't pay only money for it. Offer, along with that money, your smiling wishes for the seller's happiness. Indeed, shopping should be an exchange of good will, and not only of material goods. When you meet salespeople who give no evidence that they understand this truth, smile at them with even *greater* kindness—if only to protect yourself from their indifference. Whenever you give or pay anything, feel that, beyond that outlay, you are offering your friendship and good will.

7. Don't equate non-attachment with poverty-consciousness. Dress pleasantly—not to make yourself attractive, but to give pleasure to others. Any effort people make to improve things in this world, show them, if possible, your appreciation.

As a youth—to my mother's dismay, I'm afraid!—I used sometimes to ring the doorbells of homes that I considered particularly lovely. I thanked their owners for providing that pleasure to others. I don't say that you should go to such lengths, but I do think we all need to express our thanks and appreciation to others more often for the good that they do. As far as money-attachment is concerned, the more we give, and the less we desire money for ourselves, the more we find ourselves sustained by life itself.

8. Don't equate renunciation with negligence or with a sloppy appearance. One time in Phoenix, Arizona, Paramhansa Yogananda met a man who was unkempt, shabbily dressed, and physically unclean. "Why do you appear that way?" the Master asked.

"I'm a renunciate," the man answered, proudly.

"But you are attached all over again," answered the Master, "this time, to disorder!"

9. It is good to be practical when shopping for anything, whether it be for a shirt or for something really expensive. I have learned, however, that whatever bargaining I do works best if I make *the seller's* needs my concern also. Usually I find that he himself tries, in return, to be as fair to me as possible.

10. Realize that it is not a suitable expression of non-attachment to treat money as though it meant nothing to you. The proof of an act lies

in its consequences. Many film stars in the 1930s, for example, gave money away indiscriminately. It was more than coincidental, surely, that several of them, though wealthy at the time, died in poverty. Show respect for whatever God gives you. Don't disdain it. It doesn't please Him if you try to show non-attachment by treating His bounty carelessly. Be grateful for everything that comes to you. Share your bounty with others, in a spirit of gratitude to the Supreme Giver, but share it also with good sense.

11. Money is energy. When you need it for anything, don't wish passively that it come to you. As a renunciate, especially if you live in a monastic community, your access to funds will probably be limited. Nevertheless, never think of yourself as poor. God is the Lord of the very universe: He "owns" everything! There is *nothing* He will deny you, if you ask Him correctly.

When I lived at Mt. Washington as a monk, the allowance I received for some years was fifteen dollars a month. (Later, the amount was increased to twenty dollars.) When I was still getting fifteen dollars, it occurred to me one day that a *navaratna* (nine-gem bangle) would be spiritually helpful to me. I didn't let my extreme shortage of money (relative, certainly, to that intention) discourage me.

Nor did I ask my superiors or anyone else for financial help. I simply affirmed, with will power, that the bangle was mine already. Before long, I did get it. I sold it, years later, to help pay for Ananda.

12. Equate abundance with your real *needs*. Poverty is not lack: It is *the consciousness of lack.* Be satisfied with whatever God gives you. I have always found that with this attitude my needs, both great and small, were fulfilled.

13. Have faith. Doubt is mental static. When you ask God for anything, make a firm, loving, *demand.* Ask Him also, "Fulfill my request only if it is Your wish." Then *know* that He will respond.

14. Faith is more than belief. It is an act of conscious will. To exercise it when requesting the fulfillment of any true need, send *energy with will power* through the spiritual eye at the point between the eyebrows. Raise the energy from your heart with a pure desire to do good, then send that energy forward from the medulla to the spiritual eye. From that point, release it into the Infinite.

Visualize not so much specific results as the *direction* you want the energy to go. Your will, united to God's will, has potentially limitless power. The energy, consciously directed, will magnetically attract to you what you want.

15. Pray or affirm with will power, but always be non-attached to the results. These can be safely left in God's hands. Otherwise, you may find that what you attract is not beneficial, but harmful to you.

16. Your attitude, when seeking to manifest a desire, should be loving, grateful, and filled with joy.

17. Never tell yourself that material self-sufficiency contradicts the spirit of renunciation. Renunciation is not self-deprivation: it is an attitude that everything belongs to God. This attitude attunes your power to that of the Infinite. That is why renunciates in India are often addressed as *Maharaj*: Great King.

One who has mastered himself is, in a completely valid sense, master of the whole universe. His supremacy comes not from subjugating anybody, but from harmonizing himself with the love and joy that brought everything into existence.

XVI

Obedience

Obedience, in Western tradition, is considered the supreme monastic virtue. That tradition was given justification in several ways. First, there was some presumption that monks who rose to positions of authority were worthy of receiving obedience. (A doubtful proposition, surely.) Moreover, high position itself tended to be equated with greater holiness. Second, these "superiors" were supposed to be earthly representatives of Jesus Christ. (Wishful thinking, this rather seems.) Third, it was claimed that if a superior erred in making any directive, Christ himself would correct him. (Considering the divine silence attending a great deal of ruthless persecution in religion, this must be the most doubtful proposition of all!)

Our Guru's words on this subject give very qualified support to tradition. He taught that obedience to one's guru is certainly necessary. To obey someone who hasn't attained that level of wisdom, however, especially if the obedience is mandatory, can weaken one's will power.

Obviously, where directives are given by

unenlightened superiors there is at least the possibility that some of them may be wrong. In the war crimes trials at Nuremberg after World War II, a common excuse offered was, "I was only obeying orders." This reasoning was rejected by human courts of law. Still less should it be acceptable where spiritual rights and wrongs are the issue.

One would like to believe that monastic superiors will not order their subordinates to do anything morally reprehensible. This is the hope, but it would be foolish to inscribe that hope as a dogma. Indeed, when one thinks of the example of the Spanish Inquisition, and of numerous other evils that have been perpetrated in the name of religion—and *sanctioned* in the name of God by religious leaders—one cannot honestly support the concept that religious obedience is always holy.

Usually, of course, the issues are not black and white. Still, renunciation is supposed to help one not only to please God, but to *find* Him. Such being the case, it would be foolish to hand over the reins of one's spiritual life entirely to persons who are incompetent to give wise guidance.

When I met my Guru, he asked me to give him my unconditional obedience. I was desperately anxious to be accepted as a disciple. Nevertheless, I felt that in so vital a matter I had to be completely honest.

"What," I asked him, "if I should ever feel you to be wrong?"

His answer satisfied me completely. He said, "I will never ask anything of you that God Himself doesn't tell me to ask."

I was confident that he knew God. I was certain, therefore, that he would never betray my trust. And he never did so. Rather, I was constantly amazed at the depth of wisdom revealed in his guidance.

He was my Guru, however, and had a right to make that request of me. Later successors were not on the same spiritual level as he. The demands they made of me did not always take my spiritual needs into serious consideration.

My Guru had told me, for example, that my duty in life would be writing, lecturing, and editing. A later superior of mine had other ideas. There was a hired printer at Mt. Washington who asked that I be assigned to work with him in the print shop. The president, anxious to gratify his request, asked me if I wouldn't do so. I told her I didn't think this was the right kind of work for me, adding, "Any machinery I work on is bound to break down within a week! I just haven't a talent for it." My rejection had upset her; therefore I'd added that explanation. My Guru's instructions to me, however, had been my major concern. I was struck by the fact that those instructions hadn't been given serious consideration. Had I accepted this job, it would have meant a major change of focus for me, and one very different from what he himself had told me I must do.

What would have happened, then, had he *not* given me those instructions? I might indeed have become a printer, in violation of my true nature and in opposition to my own spiritual needs. Would the change have been good for me, justified by "holy obedience"? I doubt it.

In India, years later, the person heading our work asked me to take charge of the main office. I objected, saying, "Were I to accept that position, it would be another twenty years before I even saw the light of day again!"

"Quite right," he answered matter-of-factly.

Fortunately, again, I had my own Guru's personal instructions to guide me. What would have happened, had he not given them? I'd have had to suppress my natural inclination in soldierly obedience to a wrong directive. I would have had to go against the grain of my true nature. With God's grace, my true guru had pointed out to me what I needed to do, to fulfill not only the needs of the work, but of my own nature. I might possibly have been useful to the organization, since I did have some flair for office work. The question would have remained, however: *Would the organization have been useful to me?*

I could go further into these matters, but I think the two illustrations I've given, drawn from my own life, show the tendency of institutions to place their own convenience above the needs of individuals. These examples should suffice to show that the ideal of monastic obedience is open to serious question. The issue remains, surely, to *whom* is one being obedient? To God? All right, but I think obedience should always be tempered by common sense.

In fact, I tried earnestly for years to give to my superiors the same obedience I had given to my Guru. I did so even when I frankly didn't believe they were right. I reminded myself of St. Teresa of Avila's strict obedience to her spiritual counsellor.

Yet I learned, years later, that she'd written deprecatingly of the great spiritual harm that is done by unenlightened spiritual advisers. In any case, where less important directives were concerned I considered good-humored cooperation to be better than resistance. For I also remembered Yogananda's words in *Autobiography of a Yogi* to the effect that he himself had never been commandeered by details. It was, I decided, spiritually right to obey even minor instructions. Not only was it important to the harmony of the work we were doing: It was good also as a means of suppressing any temptation to self-will in myself. To contest a directive of minor importance would, I felt, mean displaying an uncooperative spirit, and quite pointlessly.

In time, however, I found, as I've said, that what was asked of me was sometimes a contradiction of my Guru's specifically stated instructions to me. In such cases, I could only consider it my duty to tell them what his instructions had been. Usually, where my own activities were concerned, they accepted what I said and went along with it.

Where instructions he'd given me concerned the work as a whole, however, rather than the role I was to play in it, they generally ignored what I told them. Perhaps they thought that, since he hadn't given them those instructions personally, he must not have really given them at all.

I began to ask myself, "What must I do?" My goal was to find God. Would it further me in that aim if I opposed them? I did considerable soul searching on this point, and decided that my duty was to concern myself only with what he had said personally to me *for my own* spiritual growth, and not to insist on other instructions he'd given me.

In my own work, as head of the monks, I said to them all, "I know it is customary for the monk in charge to demand obedience of those under him. I don't feel comfortable with that tradition, however. All I ask of you is your willing cooperation."

At Ananda also, the only obedience requested of resident members is willing cooperation.

The same is true, therefore, of Ananda's renunciate order. My purpose is not ever to violate anyone's free will. That is each person's divine heritage. My divine obligation to everyone who comes to me, and to Ananda, for spiritual guidance is to respect that heritage.

On the subject of obedience, therefore, I

would say only this: Be *open* to whatever guidance you are given. If you don't agree with it, state your reasons, and offer alternatives. Naturally, willing cooperation is necessary if there is to be any coherence in a community. I myself cooperate willingly with any good idea, whatever its source.

In the next chapter I will offer a few guidelines—first for those in positions of authority, and second for those who are in their charge.

XVII

The Rule of Cooperative Obedience

For Those in Positions of Authority:

1. Remember, Ananda Sangha is a *spiritual* work. Its purpose is to provide an environment for giving its members every encouragement to find God. Directives should therefore always be given with this purpose in mind.

2. Naturally, in directing the work there will be organizational needs to be filled, and persons available who are more or less qualified to meet those needs. Never ask anyone to do something, however, even if he expresses willingness to do so, that does not seem right for his spiritual growth.

   For instance—and this has actually happened—there may be a pressing need for an accountant. A member of the community may have all the necessary skills for that position. If it is evident, however, that this work would not spiritually benefit him, perhaps because it might make him devotionally dry, *do not assign that work to him.* The organization itself may suffer; have faith, nevertheless, that God Himself will provide a solution. Meanwhile, never *use* anybody.

3. Look upon everyone who serves God under you as your equal in Him. Never treat anyone with condescension.

4. It will seem strange to make a separate rule of looking at other sets of rules, but my books, *The Art of Supporting Leadership*, and, *Secrets of Leadership*, both contain many principles that will be helpful to monastic superiors.

5. Never treat anyone under you as a mere worker. Be concerned for his spiritual well-being, and *show* your concern.

6. Encourage a prayerful attitude in the work place. Have people meditate at least briefly in the morning before work begins. If anyone wants to meditate at different points during the day, encourage him to do so provided he doesn't take too much time out. Always keep before your charges the

spiritual and devotional purpose behind what you are asking them to do.

7. Keep a small altar in your work place, and see that it is garlanded every day.

8. Pray, at least briefly, before issuing any directive. Visualize the heart of the person you are directing, and try to feel whether what you intend to ask of him feels right, there, for his spiritual well-being.

For Those in Subordinate Positions:

1. Usually in monasteries, though not always, a person is in a subordinate position either because he hasn't the talent for leadership, or because he hasn't the seniority, or because he has something to learn which another can teach him. Humility is good, always. The superior should not view himself as truly superior. And the subordinate should never equate humility with submissiveness. The ideal attitude for the subordinate is an attitude of cheerful, willing cooperation.

2. The traditional teaching that one should view his superior as an instrument of Christ, or of God, is good advice, generally speak-

ing. As I said earlier, however, it is only pro-
visionally so. In fact, the true devotee sees
everyone as the Lord in human form. The
rocks themselves are manifestations of Him
who brought the whole universe into existence. If any superior preens himself in the
thought that he manifests God to others, it
means he has misunderstood it utterly.

The superior should see his subordinates,
also, as instruments of God—perhaps
through the very frustrations they cause
him! For spiritual growth, even inanimate
objects can serve as instruments of God. This
doesn't mean at all that one should be sub-
missive to everything and everyone.

One's superior in a monastery may, in fact,
be a divine test for the subordinate. One
should weigh every directive he receives
against his own joy within. Willing, cheerful
cooperation is a wonderful thing, but
should also be supported by common sense.
Right attitude is essential to spiritual maturity. The grumbling, unwilling subordinate
gains the least from his life lived for God.

3. Obviously, not every directive one
   receives from a monastic superior will be
   spiritually right. Much of the benefit

gained from obedience comes from *attitude.*

Many years ago at the SRF Lake Shrine in Pacific Palisades, a young monk was given the daily task of clambering across the steep hillsides to water the plants. Dragging a long and heavy hose about, soaking himself to the skin in the process, was so distressing to him that he actually hated the job. Yet, every morning he was given the same assignment.

After some time he awoke one morning thinking, "If this is the only job I'll ever have, I might as well enjoy it!" That morning he came cheerfully down to breakfast, ready for anything.

This turned out to be, as it happened, the day that his job changed. I think he was never given that job again. In any case, what changed the situation for him was his change of attitude.

4. It does happen, of course, that a superior makes requests that are not only unwise, but sometimes even wrong for the monk's spiritual growth. To take a strictly hypothetical case, a young monk with a romantic weak-

ness for a particular woman in his past may
be asked to attend her wedding. The superi-
or might not be aware that he had this weakness, or else he may be aware of it, but may
see this as an opportunity to help the monk
to rid himself completely of the past.
Whether the superior gives this directive
wisely, or is simply uninformed—and, it
should be added, it is generally better for
monks not to attend weddings—the monk
owes it to himself and to his relationship
with the superior to explain his situation.
Blind obedience, particularly in such matters, would be foolish.

5. If you receive a directive that you consider
   morally or spiritually wrong, don't imagine
   that obedience will absolve you of any
   blame attached to the action. You must use
   your own discrimination. In such cases, first
   calm your heart's feelings. Next, hold them
   up to the spiritual eye, and ask for guidance
   at that point. You heart's feeling will tell
   you what is right for you to do.

   Monastic obedience should always be given
   primarily to God. Don't let blind obedience weaken your moral sense. To do so
   would be a great mistake, and an even
   greater one on the part of the superior who

makes the demand of you.

6. In a religious work there are, as I've indicated before, two types of devotees: those to whom expansion of any kind is viewed with suspicion, as though reeking of delusion; and those who want to share with others what they've learned of the truth. I discount those who, out of ego-motivation, are either selfish and contractive or eager to go about converting everybody, beating drums in the hope that everyone will marvel at their zeal.

When Paramhansa Yogananda obtained Mt. Washington Estates, Laurie Pratt, his chief editor, announced, "Now your troubles begin!" In her mind, to spread the work was an exercise in futility. She told me herself that she saw no rush, even in later years, about getting all his books edited and published. "What do they need with more books?" she demanded. "They already have everything they need, to find God."

It was she who put me out of SRF. As she did so, she discouraged me from writing (as my Guru had told me to do), deprecating any such activity with the words, "What's the use? Everything has been said countless times before."

Between the contractive and the expansive types of devotees there cannot be any real understanding. If your superior is one type, and you are another, accept the situation, if you must, but be aware that you are rowing toward troubled waters. Constant struggle may lead, in time, to frustration for you both.

7. Never let an unsympathetic superior "get your goat." Be cheerful, but never surrender your own sense of what is right and wrong.

I once had a superior—not SRF's president, but another nun—who was, in my own and everyone's opinion, excessively strict and rigid. I simply would not run just because she "barked." Instead, I calmly and good-humoredly offered my own "take" on things. Usually she ended up agreeing with me. When she didn't, I was glad to see that she never took offense. She knew that she had my support.

Did I always obey her? Frankly, I'm not so sure I did. It seems to me, however, that if I did so it was always with good humor in the thought, "What does it matter, anyway? This is all God's dream. I'm not going to let myself become upset over trifles."

8. Make harmony your priority. A rebelli
spirit may win you points now and then,
but in the end it will destroy your peace of
mind and inner attunement, and will in
addition disturb others—all to no avail.
Peace and harmony are the foundations of
the spiritual life.

XVIII

How to Be an   Attitudes Detective

Watch your heart: That is where attitude reveals itself for what it is. A right attitude will lift your energy from the heart toward the spiritual eye. A wrong attitude will depress the heart's energy and pull it down toward the base of the spine. When a wrong attitude intrudes itself, you may actually feel the energy draining downward from the brain, first, and then downward from the heart. Right attitude will bring you inner harmony, peace, and contentment. Wrong attitude, on the contrary, will bring you disharmony and an inner sense of heaviness.

Attitude is the most important thing on the spiritual path. When your attitude is good, you'll be able to sail through every test—often without even realizing that it *was* a test. When your attitude is wrong, on the other hand, everything will seem to be a test. You can find in even kindly smiles some cause for irritation.

Watch the directional flow of your energy, especially in the spine. Whatever your reason tells you, if the energy moves downward, know that there is something wrong—and wrong *with you*.

As my Guru said to one of my fellow monks, "Whenever you see wrong in the world, remember, it's wrong with *you*. When you are right, everything is right, because you see God there."

XIX

Attunement

I have written so far about renunciation in a monastic setting. Many renunciates, however, do not live in monasteries. Some of them live in solitude. Some of them are wandering sadhus. And some of them live in society, but have dedicated their hearts to God.

Some people would like to live among other renunciates, but have yet to find a community that feels right to them.

I myself lived for fourteen years in the monastic setting of SRF. I did my best to fit in, for I deeply believed, and still do believe, that I was serving my Guru as he wanted me to do. My superiors in the order, however, saw things very differently. I was forced, finally, to leave and serve my Guru on my own. I am not sorry I didn't fit in. I had another mission to fulfill, one that resulted in the founding of Ananda Sangha, and in a creative outpouring that has resulted in over eighty books, over 400 pieces of music, fifteen thousand color slides, and a new, more expansive view of Paramhansa Yogananda's mission in the world.

SRF has claimed that the Master came to start a monastery. I believe I am right in stating unequivocally that they are mistaken. His mission was to the whole world: not only to monks and nuns, but to show everyone, everywhere, that the missing ingredient in life, the lack of which has produced in modern times so much world-wide suffering and turmoil, is communion with God.

I did not leap in these new directions the moment I was out of SRF. I had believed in what I was doing there. Now I questioned my very attunement with my Guru. Had I, I wondered, and despite my belief—indeed, despite my zeal for serving him—been misguided in my attunement?

My then-superiors told me never to lecture again; never to write; never to contact any member of SRF; never even to tell people I was Yogananda's disciple. I tried to do what they wanted of me. I tried to drop out, to become a silent, solitary hermit, to become unknown in the world.

Every door I approached in that search for solitude was closed in my face—by circumstances, as well as by people. What could I do? Presumption on God's guidance would have been disastrous for me at that time. I had to take a single small step at a time, then consult my heart as well as the reactions of other people. I had to see, step by step, if I was going in the right direction.

It became increasingly clear to me that my Guru and God *wanted* me to lecture, teach, and do a public work as my Guru had in fact told me I must. I tried many times to test this guidance and prove it wrong. Peace and inner joy came to me only when I followed what my Guru had told me, though his words and my own inner experience were diametrically opposed to what my superiors insisted I must do, or—in this case—not do. Indeed, had they given me *anything* to do, I'd have followed their directive unremittingly to the horizon. All they ever insisted on, however, were the things they didn't want me to do. The one thing I could *not* do as a service to him was *nothing*.

In *Autobiography of a Yogi*, when Yogananda first saw his guru Swami Sri Yukteswar standing in a narrow Benares lane, looking in his direction, Yogananda thought hungrily for a moment, "I have found him! That is my guru!" And then, to test his own feeling, he tried several times to turn and walk away. Each time he did so, his feet grew heavy, and he found himself unable to move. Whenever he turned back toward his guru, he found that he was free to move. Thus, after several attempts, he became convinced that this was no mere fancy of his: He *had* indeed found his guru, who was magnetically calling him!

In similar fashion, though with far less immediate results, I tested my inner attunement to make sure that what I felt was, truly, my Guru's guidance. My fellow disciples assumed, cynically, that I had "leapt" toward what I wanted to do. Far from it! Little by little, with great suffering in the process but driven almost relentlessly in the direction I slowly realized I must take, the guidance came to me. It came in a thousand ways: from within as well as from without.

I am confident, now, that the path I followed was the right one, and that what my superiors had ordered me not to do was determined by their own convenience, not by my spiritual needs, and not by our Guru's wishes.

Attunement, I am convinced, is the first and greatest need on the path. It is the final goal of renunciation. It is the only way to find God.

What is attunement? In the Bible, near the beginning of the Gospel of St. John, we read, "To all those who received him, to them gave he power to become the sons of God." My Guru very often repeated those words. The simple truth is, no human being can make the leap from ego-consciousness to cosmic consciousness by merely believing in that infinite consciousness. Yogananda described the attainment of this state of consciousness as "the liberating shock of omnipresence." This statement, which appears in his autobiography in the chapter on cosmic consciousness, is too overwhelming a concept to be understood by reason alone. The ego is not omnipresent even in its own little body! How can it soar from its drastic confinement to the vastness of absolute consciousness?

The essence of the spiritual path is attunement.

Devotees often insist, "God is the Guru. What need have I for a human guide?" God, however, does everything through instruments. Even the stars and planets were created by higher beings in attunement with His will. Yes, God is Omnipresence. Yes, He knows our least thought. He acts, however, through instruments. As the child needs teachers, even though all the information they teach is available to him, if he knows how to seek it, so the sincere seeker absolutely needs a guru.

God loves His human creations, and wants them to live in harmony, peace, and happiness. He will not impose His wishes on them, however, not even for their own welfare. God uses those who have found Him, not to impose His will on anyone, but to bring seeking souls back to oneness with Him. Without attunement to the guru's consciousness, the ego cannot even *think* except within the limitations of ego-consciousness!

Renunciation alone will not take anyone to God. Prayer and meditation are not enough to get you there. Nor is institutional affiliation, nor even "signing up with" the right Guru. In every great guru's ashram there are a few disciples who have achieved spiritual depth, and others who are still spiritual children. The guru shines his light equally on all his disciples, but not all of them are equally able to receive its rays.

Ultimately, *no* human effort will take us to God. The whole secret of the spiritual path is to get the ego, and the attachments and desires that cling to it like barnacles, out of the way, and to *receive* into our souls the blessings of God. What the guru does for us is primarily on a level of *consciousness.* He works *from within*, on our thoughts and feelings. Our job above all, then, is to offer our hearts and minds up to him, that he may transform us. Gradually, his ego-less consciousness seeps into our ego-centered consciousness, and transforms us with new understanding of our own reality.

The true goal of renunciation, then, is only one: to eliminate every attachment to littleness, in order that the guru may enter and expand our awareness to infinity.

For more information, to request a catalog, or to place
an order from Crystal Clarity, please contact us at:

ᛒ QᴜᴏɴᴅAᴍ

Crystal Clarity Publishers
14618 Tyler Foote Road
Nevada City, CA 95959

Toll Free: 800.424.1055 or 530.478.7600
Fax: 530.478.7610
clarity@crystalclarity.com

For our online catalog and secure ordering,
please visit us on the web at:
www.crystalclarity.com